The Four Great Railways

MICHAEL R. BONAVIA
MA, PhD, FCIT

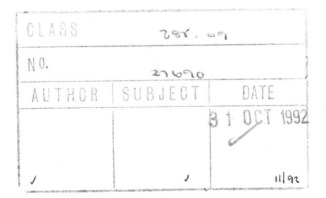
DAVID & CHARLES
NEWTON ABBOT LONDON
NORTH POMFRET (VT)

British Library Cataloguing in Publication Data

Bonavia, Michael Robert
  The four great railways.
  1. Railroads – Great Britain – History –
  20th century
  I. Title
  385'.0941   HE3018

ISBN 0 7153 7842 2

Photoset and printed in Great Britain
by Redwood Burn Limited, Trowbridge, Wilts
for David & Charles (Publishers) Limited
Brunel House Newton Abbot Devon

Published in the United States of America
by David & Charles Inc
North Pomfret Vermont 05053 USA

Contents

The maps are broadly based on the Railway Clearing House maps and show lines in the ownership of the companies before the second world war, although not at a given date. The company boundary should not therefore in all cases be taken as the limits of train services.

For reasons of scale, some of the fine detail has of necessity been omitted in such congested areas as London, West Yorkshire, Central Scotland and South Wales.

Author's Preface and Acknowledgments

It might be thought that so many railway histories have been written, and so many are still being written, that there is scarcely room for a book which sets out to deal with the four main line railways from 1923 to 1947, within a relatively small compass. But there is something of a gap, which I am endeavouring to fill, between the histories of individual companies, which frequently concentrate upon the engineering side and especially on locomotive design and performance, and those erudite studies by economic and transport historians dealing with the railway industry as a whole, mainly in terms of road-rail competition, pricing policy, investment and financial performance.

Perhaps understandably, the pre-grouping railways have attracted more attention from historians than the amalgamated companies – their enterprise and struggles, their achievements and shortcomings, are a fundamental element in that astonishing century of material progress that ended with the first world war. But railway history continued to be exciting after 1923, and I have tried to show where the grouped companies railways differed from their predecessors and where the old fighting spirit survived. If, in the process, I betray a certain partiality towards the London & North Eastern Railway, I hope I may be forgiven by those whose loyalties and pre-nationalisation origins lie elsewhere.

I am deeply grateful to former colleagues and friends who have read various chapters and made helpful criticisms and suggestions. I am particularly indebted to – in alphabetical order – D. S. M. Barrie, A. R. Dunbar, J. L. Harrington, G. R. Hayes, R. A. Long, and A. W. Tait, though a scrupulously complete list would have to be far longer. I must however emphasise that the responsibility for any remaining errors or omissions is entirely mine.

M. R. B.

Chapter 1

The Birth of the Groups

To those of us who grew up with them between the wars, the four great railways seemed part of the settled order of things, as permanent as any such institutions could be. It is sometimes hard to realise that their life-span was only twenty-five years, from 1923 to 1948. Their upstart successor, British Rail, has already had a substantially longer life; and of course their predecessors – the 'constituent' and 'subsidiary' companies swallowed up in 1923 – mostly had much longer existences.

In those twenty-five years the 'amalgamated' or 'group' companies, as they were officially termed, established firm individual characteristics. If the politicians and civil servants who drafted the Railways Act 1921 had expected uniformity to appear, they were disappointed. The railways continued to be different not merely in the liveries of locomotives and carriages; their engineering practices and their whole management styles showed considerable diversity. Admittedly, through the Railway Clearing House, where committees sat to try to agree uniform policies in freight rates and passenger fares, as well as in many other matters, it was often possible for the railways to act in unison. But both to the passenger and to the schoolboy train-spotter, the Great Western was utterly unlike, say, the LNER. There was no mistaking upon which railway one was travelling, or on whose platforms one was standing to watch the trains.

The pace at which a new railway character, different from that of the old pre-grouping companies, began to appear varied considerably. On the Great Western there was little visible change except in Wales, above all in the mining valleys and ports of South Wales. Over most of its territory

5

'God's Wonderful Railway' (as men from other lines were inclined sardonically to term it) continued its stately progress. By contrast, on the Southern, the management skill and progressive outlook of Sir Herbert Walker and his carefully picked team soon evolved the character of a new railway, quite distinct from its component systems. This was no doubt greatly assisted by the energetic programme of electrification and general physical modernisation that Walker pushed through his Board.

But the two largest companies – the LMS and the LNER – took longer to emerge with corporate identities. For some years after grouping, the characteristics of their main constituents still seemed more in evidence than any really new image. In the mid or even late 1920s, a blindfolded rail fan – in those days he would probably have been called a 'railway-ac' – taken on a tour of the London termini could probably still have identified them by nose and ear according to their pre-grouping characters, especially when a main line train was about to depart. At Paddington there was, over and above the smell of warm oil and steam, a faint odour of straw and also of spilt milk, drifting down from the mysterious lengths of platform A, inaccessible to the public, just round the curve at the departure end of platform 1, where milk churns and parcels were loaded. Then there would be the particular sizzle of the Swindon safety valve, rising to a gentle crescendo just before departure, followed by the measured beat of the exhaust as a Churchward or Collett 4–6–0 eased its train out of the station, without slipping, the driver giving only enough steam for a clean exit without pulling the fire through the tubes.

What a contrast at Euston! There the smell of spilt milk was stronger and mixed with that of fish traffic. As departure time approached, a deafening roar from the safety valves was usual, both from the train engine and also from the bank engine, far away at the buffer stops, which had brought in the empty carriages. Departure was a very noisy ceremony, usually accompanied by a good deal of slipping, as the train made its way over the point and crossing work and approached the 1 in 70 of Camden bank. As the noise of the train engine diminished, that of the banker panting furiously in the rear – probably an elderly 0–6–2T with the real 'Crewe bark' in its exhaust – would grow to a roar as it shoved and pushed all the way up the bank past Camden locomotive depot.

King's Cross again was always different. The peculiar acrid smell of South Yorkshire coal would afflict the nose, and the start was difficult before the plunge into Gas Works Tunnel; despite the adverse gradient facing the engine so soon after the start, no banking assistance was ever given at 'the Cross'.

The sights of the four great railways are well preserved in countless still photographs and many films; some of the sounds too are there on disc, though mostly recorded after nationalisation. But the smells have almost all gone – those unique blends of steam, warm oil, smoke, spilt milk, stale fish and horse manure! (One sometimes forgets that the Big Four bequeathed nearly 9000 horses to British Railways in 1948.)

In the 25 years of their existence, the four great companies had seemed to be so firmly established as eventually to justify the upheaval that had attended their creation – the compulsory merger of 120 railways into four. But, looking back, there are a number of questions that can reasonably be asked. First of all, why was it necessary – or did it seem necessary – to interfere so drastically with a rail transport system that was generally considered the best in Europe, if not in the world? And if interference *was* necessary, why not unification into a single state railway such as existed in Italy, Switzerland, Russia, Japan, and many other countries?

We must start by considering the condition of the railways just before the 1914–18 war. Among the 120 companies, the dignified top leaders – the London & North Western, which claimed to be the Premier Line, the Great Western, the

Midland and the North Eastern – were very strong financially and were also generally considered to give good service to the public. The 'second eleven' included the Great Northern, the Great Eastern, the Great Central, the London & South Western, the Caledonian, the Lancashire & Yorkshire; most were well managed, but one or two suffered from a rather weak financial position. In the third league came a number of smaller railways in England and Scotland – the London, Brighton & South Coast, the Glasgow & South Western, the South Eastern & Chatham, the North British, the Highland – and a 'tail' of such smaller concerns as the North Staffordshire, the Furness, the Great North of Scotland, and so on. This classification of course is debatable: nearly every one of the railways in the junior leagues had strong supporters and some critics. But there was a great gap between the financial strength of, say, the Midland or the North Eastern, and the shakiness of the Great Central or the Cambrian.

On the credit side, there was great company loyalty and a lot of competitive enterprise. The expression 'small is beautiful' had not been coined in 1914; but that sentiment certainly existed among the management and the staff of many railways which in the light of cold economics might have been dismissed as too small to benefit from economies of scale. Admittedly, the existence of so many small railways involved a great deal of uneconomic operation: short workings by locomotives and passenger rolling stock to frontier stations; and complicated book-keeping at the Railway Clearing House to apportion receipts from through traffic and to keep track of all wagons passing from one company's system to that of another. Above all, the obligation to return empty wagons to the parent company, as well as private owners' wagons to their base, involved a vast amount of uneconomic haulage.

Immediately before war broke out in 1914, this whole complex network of railways was taken over by the Government under the Regulation of the Forces Act 1871, and directed to operate under the instructions of the Railway Executive Committee, of which the President of the Board of Trade was nominal Chairman, but who delegated his duties to H. A. Walker, General Manager of the London & South Western Railway. For the purpose of handling the wartime traffics, the railways were managed as a single system.

The financial arrangements provided that the shareholders would be guaranteed, roughly, the 1913 net revenues: the Government would meet the expenditure and take the receipts from railway operation. The effect was that no profit could accrue to the shareholders from extra wartime traffics. Charges and wages were determined by the Government, and were no longer effectively controlled by the managements.

Not only was the whole wagon fleet placed in common-user – obviating the need to return empty wagons to an owner's siding or to a parent company, and enabling them to be loaded to any destination for which a load was available – but locomotives were freely loaned from companies with surplus power to those which were hard pressed.

The lesson, that substantial economies could be obtained by getting away from traditional independence and operating the railways more or less as a single system, was learnt both by railway managers and by outside observers

Transport was seen to be a vital factor in winning the war; although it was not then questioned that railways would continue to be the major form of inland transport in the foreseeable future, new ideas about the post-war world included new thoughts on transport organisation. Only four months after the war ended, the Government introduced a Bill into Parliament to set up a Ministry of Ways and Communications. In the House of Commons the Government spokesman said that 'some measure of unified control of all systems of transportation is necessary . . . it is only the State, only the Government that can centrally take that position'.

How close in fact did the railways come to being nationalised after the first world war? Government policy took shape, as it often does, in three stages – a report, a White Paper and a Bill. First, a Select Committee on Transport had been appointed by the House of Commons in 1918 and it reported 'that the organisation of the transport agencies of the country – and particularly of the railways – cannot be allowed to return to its pre-war position'. But the report went on to say that the wartime control arrangements would *not* be satisfactory as a permanent settlement, although 'unification of the railway system is desirable under certain safeguards, whether the ownership be in public or private hands'.

It is perhaps worth mentioning that at this time the post-war financial crisis of the railways had not yet appeared. In 1918 the railways had a net revenue of £44 millions. There was no need for immediate panic action, as was the case in 1921 when the railways had plunged into deficit through no fault of their own. By then, as Sir Felix Pole, General Manager of the GWR, wrote bitterly some years after, 'Seven years of Government control had reduced the railways from relatively prosperous commercial concerns to a precarious financial position'. Between 1913 and 1921 (when control finally ended) the railway wage bill had been increased under Government direction by 268 per cent. The Government had also conceded an eight-hour working day.

These concessions may well be regarded as justified, but until 1920 no corresponding authority was given by the Government to the railways to increase freight rates and charges, despite the plea of the Railway Executive Committee that railway charges, in common with those in every other industry, should rise to reflect increased costs. The effect was that the controlled railways, which in 1913 had had net receipts of £45.6 millions, by 1921 were running at an actual loss – which for the eight months of that year up to the end of Government control amounted to £21.6 millions. This was the railways' reward for carrying record traffics throughout the war period.

The Government's Bill to set up a Ministry of Ways and Communications changed its title during its passage through

Parliament and emerged as the Ministry of Transport Act, 1919; and that was the name the new Ministry enjoyed when it was set up, in September 1919. Everything seemed to point in the direction of nationalisation. Nine months before, Mr Winston Churchill, in a speech to the Dundee Chamber of Commerce, had said: 'Railways in private hands must be used for immediate direct profit, but it might pay the State to run railways at a loss to develop industries and agriculture.'

The widespread debates about transport were also reflected in two other events in 1919 – the incorporation by Royal Charter of the Institute of Transport, and the founding of what has become an influential weekly journal, *Modern Transport*.

The next stage was marked by the issue of a White Paper, towards the end of 1920, outlining the way in which the Government's thinking had crystallised into favouring a grouping of the railways. This contained a startling new proposal, set out as follows:

> Each of the grouped railways will require a Board of Management, and in order to secure efficiency and uniformity, and to avoid undue cost, the number of members composing the Board should be limited to probably 21 . . . composed of representatives
> (a) of the shareholders, who should form a majority on the Board, and of whom a proportion should hold large trading interests; and
> (b) of employees, of whom one-third might be leading administrative officials of the group, to be co-opted by the rest of the Board, and two-thirds members elected from and by the workers on the railway.

This was pretty revolutionary stuff for that time. Worker directors were virtually unknown in British industry, and nearly sixty years later their appointment is still the subject of hot debate. And putting functional railway officers on the Boards was equally unknown, though it would have foreshadowed to some extent the creation of the short-lived Railway Executive of 1948.

The White Paper's proposals were strongly opposed by the Railway Companies Association, representing the Boards and shareholders. To the Government's discomfiture, moreover, the proposals were also disliked by the railway unions who, while favouring in principle the creation of a State-owned and State-controlled railway system on which they would expect to have at least a 50 per cent control, were *not* impressed by the offer of a minority share on the private boards of directors.

The companies and the railway trade unions therefore met in May 1921 and agreed to ask the Government to drop the idea of worker directors, in favour of a statutory machinery of joint consultation between management and unions, over and above the negotiating machinery on wages and conditions of service that was already in existence.

The Government reluctantly agreed to backtrack and to refrain from asking Parliament to make a provision which neither the companies nor the employees desired. It issued a second White Paper announcing this decision and describing the statutory joint consultation machinery which was to be included in the Railways Bill.

In the arguments about future organisation and control of the railways, the personality of the first Minister of Transport, Sir Eric Geddes, was a major factor. Eric Campbell Geddes had had a spectacular career as a railwayman, a civil servant and a Minister of the Crown. Born in India, he worked for a time on the Baltimore & Ohio Railroad in the USA and on some Indian railways; he then joined the North Eastern Railway in the not (apparently) very exalted post of Claims Agent in 1904. Thereafter his progress was spectacular – in seven years he had become successively Deputy Chief Goods Manager, Chief Goods Manager and Deputy General Manager. Robert Bell, for long Assistant General Manager of the LNER, later commented with a touch of acidity upon Geddes's great 'ability to master the intricacies of a fresh subject and . . . his flair for magnifying his own standing in the process'.

Soon after the first world war broke out, the North Eastern Railway, which had something of a plethora of management talent, agreed to release Geddes to the Ministry of Munitions, where he became Deputy Director of Munitions Supply. Here his energy and ability greatly impressed Lloyd George, then Minister of Munitions. In consequence when Lloyd George became Prime Minister, Geddes became Director-General of Military Railways (and an honorary major-general); then Controller of the Admiralty (and an honorary vice-admiral); he then took a seat in Parliament and became First Lord of the Admiralty. On the Armistice being signed in November 1918, Geddes was entrusted with the co-ordination of the demobilisation of men from the Forces.

Cecil J. Allen in his admirable history of the LNER has given a vivid pen-picture of Geddes, in which he quotes Lloyd George's own first impression of the railway tycoon, then aged 39. 'He had the make of their [the North Eastern Railway's] powerful locomotives. That is the impression he gave me when one morning he rolled into my room. He struck me immediately as a man of exceptional force and capacity . . . he turned out to be one of the most remarkable men whom the State called to its aid in this anxious hour for Britain and her Empire'.

In all this rapid succession of important posts Geddes had taken with him assistants whom he knew and trusted from the North Eastern Railway. Very soon after the Armistice, most of the railway officers whose services had been lent to the Government returned to the railways; but the Cabinet decided to ask for the continuing services of Sir Eric Geddes (as he had become; KCB, GCB and CBE in addition) for the post of the first Minister of Transport. This raised a problem, in that Geddes was still nominally an officer of the NER, and there had been a clear understanding that he would in due course succeed to the post of General Manager when Sir Alexander Kaye Butterworth retired. It was solved by an agreement that in consideration of a lump sum payment of

£50,000, Geddes would sever all connection with the NER.

A man of Geddes's dynamism is not likely to be universally beloved, and some North Eastern men were rather relieved at his permanent departure from the railway scene. But the new Minister of Transport, as Robert Bell recorded, 'began to staff his department as though it were going to run the railways from Whitehall'. For instance, he recruited as Director of Transport (Accounting) William V. Wood who was eventually to become President of the LMS Railway, as well as other high-flyers.

But Geddes's main task was the drafting of the Act that was to settle the future shape of the railways, and the Government had by 1920 committed itself to grouping rather than unification. Until that was done, Government control was continued.

So, whatever Geddes's ambitions may have been to become supremo of all the railways as a permanent post-war job, the Coalition Government that survived until 1922 was not going to demand public ownership (no matter what Winston Churchill, still something of an *enfant terrible*, might say). Rationalisation – the stimulus of efficiency through mergers, still under private enterprise – was in favour. But a single huge corporation would have to be decentralised through some form of regional or divisional management. If this were on a purely geographical basis, it would involve protracted and complicated arrangements for transfer of management responsibilities. It was simpler and quicker to take over the existing company organisations and group them to obtain a flying start for the new set-up, while still obtaining the economies of scale and strengthening the financially weaker companies by associating them with the stronger.

While the Bill was being drafted there were consultations with a Railway Advisory Committee that had replaced the wartime Railway Executive Committee. It included twelve general managers and four trade union general secretaries. The discussions, including those with the chairmen, examined several possible methods of grouping. One involved merely hanging the minor railways on the back of a dozen or so existing major companies. Another envisaged one or possibly two groups for Scotland, and five for England. The Great Western and the Southern would have been set up as they eventually emerged but the other three in England would have comprised a London & North Western group including the Lancashire & Yorkshire plus the minor railways in the area; an Eastern/North Eastern group, including the Great Northern, the North Eastern and the Great Eastern; and a Midland and Great Central group.

With hindsight, one may consider that the pattern of six groups would have been better than the one finally adopted. It would have avoided the internecine war between ex-LNWR and ex-MR elements that hampered the new LMS for so long. Of course, the Great Central would have had short shrift from Derby, perhaps even anticipating BR's closure of the GCR London Extension some 45 years later!

But the idea of a separate group for Scotland or alternatively two Scottish groups, one Western and one Eastern, was dropped, because it was argued that the Scottish railways as a whole would constitute too weak a financial unit to obtain the investment they required. It was felt to be essential for them to be associated with English partners – a doubtful conclusion, in view of the creation of a Scottish Region for BR immediately after nationalisation!

Although the Act enforced grouping, not all the fish were swept into the net. Companies left out included all the railways that were subsequently to be incorporated in London Transport, including that 'trunk line in miniature' as it loved to style itself, the Metropolitan Railway. The Mersey Railway was left out; so too was the tiny Kent & East Sussex Light Railway. The joint lines of course were reduced in number, because many of them fell automatically into one group embracing both the parent companies, but plenty remained, the most important being the Cheshire Lines

(LMS and LNER); the Somerset and Dorset (LMS and SR); and the Midland & Great Northern (LMS and LNER). It is interesting that when the railways were finally nationalised in 1948, the Transport Act listed no fewer than fifty-nine 'railway bodies whose undertakings are transferred' – to become part of British Railways.

As the four groups emerged, although they were supposed to be based on natural associations of companies, it was not possible to distinguish any single principle behind the amalgamations. In some areas – such as South Wales – former competing railways were merged so as to create a virtual regional monopoly. In other parts of the country, competition was maintained along major traffic arteries. If one lists the main routes radiating from London, one finds that there was strong competition to Birmingham, Manchester, Sheffield, Leeds, Bradford, Edinburgh, Aberdeen, Leicester, Nottingham, and Exeter. On the other hand, a single group monopolised the services from London to Bristol, South Wales, Liverpool, Glasgow, Newcastle, York, Norwich, Dover, Brighton, Portsmouth, Southampton. In other words, the historical service patterns built up from the competition and the amalgamations of the former companies in the 19th century were largely perpetuated in the grouping, in consequence of the decision to merge companies without redeploying the assets and the managements, as was subsequently done under nationalisation.

The Railways Act 1921 as it emerged from Parliament prescribed the creation of a Southern Group, to consist of five constituent companies (LSWR, LBSCR, SER, LCDR, SECR Managing Committee) and fourteen subsidiary companies. (It was a peculiarity that the SECR was a statutory body for operating the system as a whole, but it had no shareholders; the two components and former competitors up to the year 1899, the SER and the LCDR, remained in being and in fact owned the two railway systems, the net receipts being divided in fixed proportions by the Managing Committee.)

The Western Group contained seven constituent companies of which the Great Western was infinitely the most important – the others comprising the Cambrian and some South Wales coal and dock railways. In fact, the Great Western Railway, alone among the pre-amalgamation companies, preserved continuity through the grouping, being the only one to be nominated as an 'amalgamated company'. Its twenty-six subsidiary companies included such little-known names as the Lampeter, Aberayron & New Quay Light Railway.

The North Western, Midland and West Scottish Group contained among its eight constituent companies some great names that formed strange bedfellows. The London & North Western and the Lancashire & Yorkshire in fact amalgamated voluntarily a year before the appointed date; but then there was the Midland, the North Western's great rival, while the Caledonian was thrown in together with its old enemy, the Glasgow & South Western. The minor constituents included the 'Knotty' – the North Staffordshire; the Furness; and the Highland. There were no fewer than twenty-seven subsidiary companies in all.

The North Eastern, Eastern and East Scottish Group comprised seven constituents of which the first to be named in the Act was of course the North Eastern Railway, followed by the Great Central, the Great Eastern, the Great Northern, the Hull & Barnsley, the North British and the Great North of Scotland. The subsidiary companies numbered 26.

The question of naming the new groups received considerable attention. No problem arose over the Great Western – the creation of Brunel, Gooch and Saunders survived unchanged. For the Southern Group, the name 'Southern Railway' seemed natural and was soon accepted. But the North-Western, Midland and West Scottish Group presented problems. 'London, Midland & Northern' was once favoured but Scottish susceptibilities were affronted and eventually the form 'London, Midland & Scottish' was found acceptable.

Even more difficulty arose with the North Eastern, Eastern and East Scottish Group. The title 'Great North Railway Company' was favoured for a time against 'North East Railway Company', but eventually 'London & North Eastern' was agreed; it appeased the NER element but was less acceptable in Scotland where, as Mr Hamilton Ellis has related, an old engineman complained to him that the title should have been 'London & North British'!

It was rumoured that Geddes, despite his golden handshake, still hankered for a return to railway work and in particular for the Chairmanship of a group in which the North Eastern Railway might be expected to take the lead. Against this possibility, there was a closing of the ranks among the Boards concerned!

The Railways Act 1921 has been heavily criticised by transport students and historians. At the time, it may have seemed statesmanlike; now we know that it was legislating for conditions that were rapidly passing away. It set up an Amalgamation Tribunal to oversee the machinery by which the grouped companies were to be set up; it linked profits with charges on a sliding scale and it fixed the principle of a standard revenue for each railway – which in the event was never to be earned because of the combined effects of road competition and prolonged economic depression in the heavy industries.

If those who drafted the Act with such care could have foreseen that the new companies would endure only for 25 years before being unified and nationalised as British Railways, one wonders whether they would not have scrapped the whole idea and either left the railways in their 1914 form, or nationalised them forthwith. In the event, on 1 January 1923, the appointed day under the Railways Act, the new companies came into being. Not all the amalgamations and absorptions were completed on that date; some had already been carried out, others were delayed owing to difficulties. But for all practical purposes the four great railways embarked on that date upon their quarter-century of existence – twenty-five years of enterprise and struggle. Perhaps a whole generation would have been the poorer without experience of the LMS, the LNER, the GWR and the Southern; perhaps it would have been better to have taken one bite at the cherry instead of four.

Chapter 2

The LMS and Power Struggles

The LMS (those relatively euphonious initials were soon adopted by the London Midland & Scottish Railway after short trials of LM&SR and LMSR) was a giant among railways. Its problems were also giant-sized, and they persisted, to some extent, until the end of the company's life. It was a powerful corporation, never quite so penned in the financial straitjacket in which the penury of the LNER kept that company. It included strong and very diverse personalities among its chief officers; it was no place for weaklings. It also paid the highest salaries to its chief officers and gave them the best pensions.

Boring though statistics may be, a few are necessary to show just how big the LMS was. When it was born in 1923, its route-mileage was 6,900 – or 60 per cent of the total mileage of British Railways in 1977. It had over 10,200 steam locomotives – which unfortunately cannot be meaningfully compared with the diesel and electric traction units of today – and well over 19,600 passenger carriages (against British Rail's 16,700 in 1977). Even more significantly, perhaps, it had over 207,200 freight wagons (BR in 1977 had only 166,900) and, above all, a staff, in the March 1924 census, of over 274,500, or substantially *more* than British Rail in 1977. An exact comparison is not possible because some railway activities have been hived off since nationalisation, for example road collection and delivery.

All this constituted a single railway, managed from a single head office in London, and not through five regions, each with a general manager, like BR today. It was often compared with the Pennsylvania Railroad in the USA, or with great industrial enterprises such as Imperial Chemical Industries Ltd. It was sometimes claimed to be the largest private enterprise business in the world, only exceeded in size by such state concerns as the Post Office or the Deutsche Reichsbahn (German State Railways) of the 1930s.

So the LMS was huge, centralised and autocratic. Everything it did was done in a big way – and this applied to its mistakes as well as to its successes. More than any other British railway company in the late 1920s and the 1930s, it adopted the techniques of outside big business. It pioneered the use of modern production methods in its workshops. It developed an acute sense of economics, ranging from cyclic diagramming of locomotives to cutting down the size (and the quality) of office paper to the absolute minimum – even below it!

The birth of the LMS had not been a smooth or very rapid event. Of its eight constituent companies no fewer than four represented pairs of old enemies, long separated by commercial rivalry as well as by differences of managerial outlook. In England the North Western and the Midland, in Scotland the Caledonian and the Glasgow & South Western, had a long-standing tradition of hostility.

The differences between the LNWR and the Midland were not purely commercial. The North Western, which loved to be called 'The Premier Line', prided itself upon a gentlemanly, conservative outlook. Its autocratic Chairman from 1861 to 1891, R.H. (Sir Richard) Moon, used to deliver a homily to newly appointed officers in these words: 'Remember, first, that you are a gentleman; remember, next, that you are a North Western officer and that whatever you promise you must perform – therefore, be careful what you promise, but having promised it, be careful that you perform it.' The North Western also had 'cadets' or management trainees, originally called 'runners', as early as the 1880s, long preceding the

North Eastern's traffic apprenticeships for university graduates.

The conservative side of Moon had been shown by his dislike of speed – 40 mph was his idea of an absolute maximum – and his horror of increasing train mileage in the course of timetable revision. The contrast with the Midland was remarkable. That line, although the greater part of its income came from freight, had always believed in treating its passengers well; it had pioneered third-class accommodation on all trains, Pullman sleeping cars, and upholstered seats in the third class. It had demonstrated a typical Victorian boldness in carrying through large projects such as the extension to London, the building of St Pancras Station and the construction of the Settle & Carlisle line as an independent route to Scotland – in marked contrast to the cautious LNWR policy of slow growth through amalgamations. Equally, the Midland was less 'gentlemanly', more aggressive and down-to-earth, than its rival.

It was inevitable that there should be internal power struggles in the new company and that the balance would swing first in the direction of one former constituent railway's practice, and then away again as individuals with different backgrounds rose to positions of authority. In the years after amalgamation, one very senior railway officer wrote:

> Euston appeared bent on welding the whole of the parts firmly together and setting up a large administrative headquarters to run the whole outfit. It would appear that the parts did not come together without a good deal of creaking and groaning. There are many tales of victimisation or favouritism, and though most are probably untrue or exaggerated, there does seem at times to have been a neglect of the human element. The varying ascendancy of the Derby, Hunt's Bank, or Euston schools of thought was undoubtedly painful to those not at the moment enjoying it.

E.W. Arkle in 'The Journal of Transport History', May 1962.

The initial battle was the one to secure satisfactory financial terms for the shareholders through the basis of exchange of LMS stocks for those of the companies to be amalgamated, and was in some cases protracted. The Railways Act 1921 had laid down 1 January 1923 as the appointed day upon which the new groups would come into existence, hopefully with their new capital structures completed. This was not possible in all cases; the Caledonian Railway's terms were only agreed by the tough negotiators of that proud Scottish concern months later.

Curiously enough, a voluntary amalgamation between the London & North Western and the Lancashire & Yorkshire railways had been carried out amicably with effect from 1 January 1922, ante-dating the formal grouping by a year. Although the L&Y's name disappeared after the merger, it did not seem to outside observers as though the larger company had swallowed the smaller, rather the reverse. Lancashire & Yorkshire men took over the jobs of the General Manager, the Secretary and the Chief Mechanical Engineer, as well as other senior posts, in the newly enlarged LNWR.

There were two main reasons for this – early deaths and a shortage of management talent in the top echelons of the North Western in the immediate post-war years, and at lower levels, the LNWR's gentlemanly tradition had meant that an abnormally large number of its cadets and junior officers had volunteered for service in the Forces – considerably more, as a proportion of the grades involved, than on either the L&Y or the Midland Railway, for instance. Some were killed and some did not return to the railway.

Accordingly, at the formation of the LMS the LNWR was already equipped with a General Manager, Sir Arthur Watson and a CME, George Hughes, from the 'Lanky' – not to mention the redoubtable Ashton Davies, Superintendent of the Northern Division and other strongly individual characters such as T. W. Royle, Assistant Superintendent of the same Division, both the last-named becoming Vice-

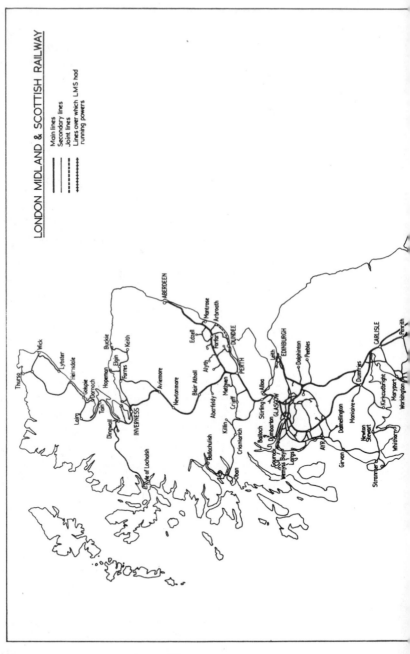

LONDON MIDLAND & SCOTTISH RAILWAY

Main lines
Secondary lines
Joint lines
Lines over which LMS had
running powers

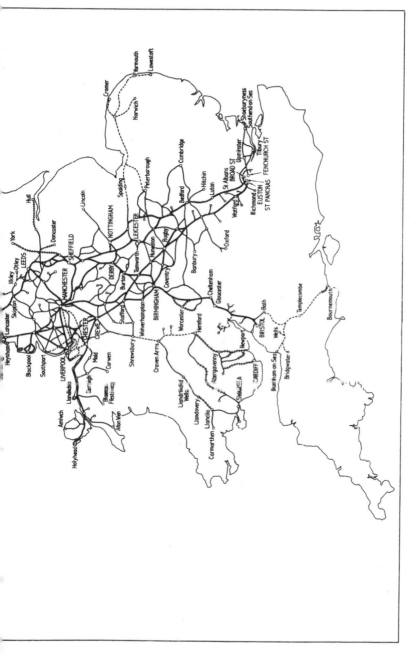

Presidents of the LMS in course of time.

But the Midland was in no way overshadowed by the LNWR/LYR coalition – quite the contrary. The first LMS Chairman, Sir Guy Granet, was himself an ex-Midland General Manager. The whole operating concept on the new system was standardised upon that of the Midland. There, the immense volume of slow-moving and often unpunctual freight traffic, especially coal, had previously been subject to serious complaints about the service, while there had been wasteful, unplanned use of locomotive power and, often, excessive working hours for train crews. Starting around 1907, modern methods of train control had begun in a small way with an office at Rotherham (Masboro') at which telephone links with signal-boxes and staff booking-on points were established. Soon this system, originated by the General Superintendent, Cecil Paget, that able if sometimes wayward genius – son of a Midland Company chairman – in conjunction with J.H. Follows, a later Vice-President of the LMS, was to be developed and spread to the whole of the Midland Railway, where it led to the establishment of a central control at Derby working directly with no fewer than 26 District Control Offices. Critics said that it was over-centralised. It certainly was very different from the North Western system of relatively large Districts having a fair degree of independent authority. But it vastly improved punctuality and effected substantial economies on the Midland, and it was not surprising that it was transplanted to the LMS under Follows (Paget having retired in 1919 to enter industry), with, not unnaturally, some heart-burnings among the non-Midland portions of the new system.

The struggles for power among the giant constituents brushed aside the claims of smaller railways such as the Furness and the North Staffordshire, even though classed as constituents and not subsidiaries. They became in effect the Barrow District and the Stoke District, and had to toe the line laid down by headquarters. In Scotland, the proud Caledonian, with its splendid, highly individual character, from the blue livery of its sturdy locomotives to the hanging flower baskets at many of its neat, well maintained stations, fought hard to maintain its individuality, with a measure of success. The 'Caley' dominated the new system in Scotland, partly no doubt because it provided in the shape of its last General Manager, Donald Mathieson, a Deputy General Manager (Scotland), for the group. Later the post was re-designated Chief Officer (Scotland).

But the Caley's traditional enemy, the Glasgow & South-Western, certainly lost out in the amalgamation, while the Highland, always dependent upon the southern companies for much of its through traffic, was easily digested, although retaining a certain independence of spirit, perhaps fostered by remoteness and a severe climate!

The speed at which the engines of the constituent companies were scrapped in the first 10 years after amalgamation gives some hint of their position in the power struggle. The LNWR and the Midland lost just under and just over 40 per cent respectively. The Caledonian lost just under 13 per cent; but the poor Glasgow & South Western almost 80 per cent! This could no doubt be justified on purely engineering grounds, but it is a symbol of the 'Sou' West's' eclipse.

The history of the LMS really falls into three periods. The first comprises the unsettled early years until 1926, under the general managerships of first, Sir Arthur Watson (ex- L&Y) and then of the Rt. Hon. H.G. Burgess (ex-LNWR). The second comprises the 'Stamp regime', starting in 1926 when Sir Josiah Stamp was appointed President of the Executive, and ending with the death of Lord Stamp (as he had become) in an air raid in April 1941. The third is really only a post-script, covering the Presidency of Sir William V. Wood, Stamp's successor, during the remainder of the war years and lasting until nationalisation in 1948.

It cannot be said that the first three years of the LMS were distinguished by the emergence of the new railway as some-

thing distinct from and greater than the sum of its constituents. On the contrary, policy seemed, despite high-level
directives from Euston, to be vacillating in its effects at
ground floor level. Midland red became the standard livery
for locomotives and passenger carriages, but resistance to
change in other, more vital aspects of the railway, continued.
Euston, as Hamilton Ellis has well said in his history of the
LMS, fully retained its LNWR atmosphere of 'shabby pride'.
Although there was considerable re-shuffling of locomotives,
often on an experimental basis, between the lines of the
former constituents, in essentials a journey from Euston to
Glasgow or from St Pancras to Leeds in 1925 remained very
much a trip on the North Western or the Midland respectively. The prospect of standardising locomotive design on
Lancashire & Yorkshire practice was short-lived; the Hughes
4–6–0 express passenger engines, sluggish in their original
design but good work-horses as modified with superheater
and Walschaerts valve gear, did spread southward but never
proliferated very extensively. In fact, during Hughes's short
tenure of office a substantial order was placed for the construction of Midland type 4–4–0 compound locomotives – a
design originally introduced nearly a quarter of a century
earlier.

The LMS can only be said to have emerged as a real entity,
not just a collection of systems chafing under the existence of
a single head office, after it entered its second phase. Well
before January 1923, the future Chairman, Granet, had been
dissatisfied with the quality of management talent at the top
level available within the constituents of the new company
and had approached Sir Herbert Walker of the London &
South Western, the outstanding railwayman of his day, and a
former LNWR officer. Walker had turned down the offer.
Granet now looked outside the railways altogether, after
Watson and Burgess had served their short terms, and found
a director of Imperial Chemical Industries (ICI) who was
also an ex-Civil Servant and a brilliant writer and lecturer on

economics. Equally distinguished as industrialist, academic and public official, Sir Josiah Stamp easily topped the list of 'the good and the great' who were available. But he did not become general manager of the LMS; his ICI experience had brought him into contact with big business in the USA and he was impressed by the American type of organisation under which policy was determined by a company president assisted by a small number of functional vice-presidents, each usually co-ordinating the work of a group of departments but not involved in the details of management.

The Stamp era on the LMS opened by stages. Stamp himself joined, as President of the Executive, in January 1926. He built up his Executive Committee of four Vice-Presidents in the period up to March 1927, when the retirement of H.G. Burgess as General Manager took effect (the overlapping of two nominally chief executive officers must have been a trying time), and the edifice was completed when Stamp, in addition to the Presidency, took over from Sir Guy Granet the Chairmanship of the Company in October 1927.

The new 'power house' of the LMS, the Executive Committee, consisting of the President and the Vice-Presidents, soon began to give the outside world the impression of a tough organisation that knew where it was going. Stamp himself, genial yet puritanical (he was a lifelong teetotaler and non-smoker, in marked contrast to many of his senior officers) had the same facility as a later railway tycoon who also came from ICI, Dr (Lord) Beeching, for asking apparently simple yet fundamental questions that no one had hitherto bothered to answer. Just as Beeching asked blandly for figures showing the margin of profit on each section of line and each type of service, so Stamp is reported, early on, to have asked why, when the heavy express passenger trains on the LNER and the GWR were almost invariably hauled by a single locomotive, the main trains out of and into Euston and St Pancras were so often double-headed. The economics of this practice seemed clearly unfavourable. Unimpressed by the answers he received, he put pressure on Sir Henry Fowler from the Midland, who had succeeded Hughes as CME in 1925, to produce a powerful main line passenger locomotive as a standard design, and quickly.

The story has often been told how Fowler – really a production engineer and not a designer at all – enlisted the help of both the North British Locomotive Company and his counterpart on the Southern Railway, to evolve the Royal Scot class of 4–6–0s in 1927. They were impressive looking machines with their huge boilers (Fowler, as a foreman at Derby once remarked when the CME was inside a firebox bashing away with a hammer, was 'a great man for boilers'). But their performance, though just adequate, fell much below the level attained subsequently after fairly extensive rebuilding.

Despite the existence of an impressive management team, the standard of express passenger train services under the LMS was not very creditable for quite a long time after the amalgamation. The *Railway Magazine* in 1929 published an analysis of the fastest times between London and the leading traffic centres in the provinces in the summer of that year, compared with the fastest pre-war times of 1914. The LMS came out worst of the four main lines, the average times being 2.86 per cent slower than in 1914. Comparable figures for the other railways were: LNER, 1.12 per cent slower; Southern, 0.65 per cent faster; Great Western, 3.18 per cent faster. Even in 1935, while the Western Division of the LMS was, on a similar analysis of train services, now 9.09 per cent faster than in 1914, the important Anglo-Scottish West Coast services were 0.58 per cent slower, and the Midland Division as a whole was 0.89 per cent slower than in 1914.

But if operating practice for some years lagged behind, the rationalisation and modernisation of the LMS workshops was an achievement of which the railway could well be proud. It was, for instance, claimed that a locomotive's heavy repair could be carried out in 46 working hours at Crewe Works, where formerly up to 60 days had been scheduled for this operation. The reorganisation of carriage building by the methods of unit assembly of accurately machined timber body components, pioneered by the Midland Railway, achieved similar results at Derby. The costs of construction and repair of locomotives and rolling stock were brought down dramatically by these methods.

Again, in the study of handling methods in goods stations, the LMS led the way in 1933 by engaging an industrial consultant to undertake what in later years would have been termed a work study investigation into means of improving labour productivity and service reliability.

Stamp's régime on the LMS is always associated with his sponsorship of W. A. (Sir William) Stanier as the right Chief Mechanical Engineer to end the sterile bickering between Crewe and Derby and at last to equip the railway with an adequate fleet of standard types of locomotive that could meet all the demands of the operating department. Stamp was undoubtedly determined to get the traction policy on to a much better footing, and the construction of the Royal Scots, forced upon Sir Henry Fowler, had been only a stop-gap measure. Fowler was not the man to eliminate the Kilkenny-cat warfare of Crewe and Derby; only an outsider with a good track record could do that. As the LMS operators had been vastly impressed by a 1926 experience with the GWR's *Launceston Castle*, which had been borrowed for test running over the West Coast main line, it was natural to get hold of Stanier, at that time Principal Assistant to Collett, the Great Western's CME. Stanier's success in fulfilling the remit given him by Stamp is a matter of history.

Stanier's locomotive building policy, which it is not appropriate to recapitulate here, enabled E. J. (later Sir Ernest) Lemon as Vice-President in charge of operating (a post to which he had succeeded after a brief spell as CME between Fowler's departure and Stanier's arrival), to plan radical improvements in train running. As early as 1932 there was an important measure of acceleration of principal services on the

31

Western (LNW) Division. By the mid-1930s the new strength in motive power was available. The enterprise of the LNER in introducing the streamlined Silver Jubilee High Speed Train (as it was officially termed), followed by the Coronation, stimulated the LMS to reply with the Coronation Scot, reaching Glasgow in 6½ hours at an average speed of 61.7 mph. In 1937 a further overhaul of timetables took effect, setting a norm of 60 mph for LMS expresses between all important centres; in the Midland Division in particular the pre-war timings were not merely restored but improved upon.

The years 1937–39 were the peak of performance so far as LMS train running was concerned. They ended all too soon with the outbreak of war and, only 18 months later, the death in an air raid of Lord Stamp, his wife and eldest son.

The third phase of LMS history, under Sir William Wood as President from 1941 to 1947, was dominated by wartime and immediate post-war conditions. Sir William Wood had been a splendid *éminence grise* behind Stamp, but he was not suited to the limelight. Often described as a wizard with figures, he was at his best on paper; he spoke very rapidly and quietly with a pronounced Ulster brogue and a cigarette invariably in his mouth, so that few of his hearers knew what he had said. None the less, he had a great interest in every aspect of railway work and could be frank and outspoken. His personal qualities and keen brain brought him support from his officers but he really had no chance to initiate any major policy before the demise of the LMS.

If Sir William Wood's Presidency was something of a post-script to the main history of the LMS, there was a PPS in the brief tenure of the office by G. L. Darbyshire in the last months before nationalisation. Wood had been appointed a Member of the future British Transport Commission, and left the LMS to assist in planning the BTC's role. Darbyshire had been Chief Officer for Labour and Establishment, and latterly a Vice-President; he was also to be designated the first Chief Regional Officer of the London Midland Region of British

Railways. So it was appropriate for him to take over at Euston and prepare the way.

The last Chairman, Sir Robert Burrows, was also in a caretaking capacity, since when he took over from Lord Royden in mid-1946 the virtual inevitability of nationalisation was evident. He was, however, much concerned with guiding the anti-nationalisation campaign run by the Railway Companies Association.

The LMS, like the other companies, had formed impressive paper plans. One of these had been particularly interesting; it was a proposal for a net receipts pool with the LNER and for exchange of penetrating lines, that might have had interesting results; but in the interim years 1945–47, the return towards pre-war travel standards was slow despite all those plans on paper.

Looking back over its 25 years of existence, the LMS was so closely identified with Stamp and his changing teams of Vice-Presidents that it seems appropriate to try to sum up the qualities and the shortcomings of the 'Stamp era'. To begin with, Stamp's attitude, like that of Beeching 30 years later, seems to have been that railways, although very large organisations, are not essentially different from other large businesses and that similar criteria of efficiency can be applied to them. This is, if more than a half-truth, still not the full truth. A service industry such as a railway derives its efficiency more from that intangible thing, staff morale, than any other single source. Here the intellectuality of Stamp and the tough efficiency of some of his Vice-Presidents were not always sufficient to overcome the disadvantages of remote, authoritarian control. The centralised organisation gave the impression that the bosses were pretty autocratic, and the staff clerks who exercised the personnel function were often bureaucratic and small-minded, or so it seemed, in interpreting the regulations. Juniors in some departments were not encouraged to express their views or offer suggestions. The remoteness of authority meant that, while it was outwardly respected, it was often

33

secretly criticised.

Efforts were made, after a time, to counteract this tendency by introducing a staff suggestions scheme. Other measures were the staff newspapers for the Commercial and Operating Departments and the competitions instituted (with rewards) for improved performance in, for instance, punctuality.

The LMS was good at self-defence. Sometimes this took the shape of demonstrating the existence of paper plans, as substitutes for action. E. W. Arkle, in the article already quoted, wrote from his later experience as a chief officer at Euston that 'none of the companies had a more lavish provision on paper for passenger station modernisation than the LMS, and none bequeathed a larger backlog of relics to British Railways'. It was whispered that the New Works Department secretly enjoyed setting standards for financial justification of schemes that were practically guaranteed to prevent the reconstruction of *any* passenger station. Indeed, Leeds (City) was almost the only really large LMS station to be rebuilt completely between the wars. Many other structures – Camden Goods for instance – were incredibly dirty and outdated; yet somehow they survived, year after year.

And the LMS was surprisingly unprogressive in some other respects. It seemed profoundly uninterested in electrification, except in a very limited way for suburban traffic. It inherited from the LNWR the London electrified lines from Euston to Watford and from Broad Street to Richmond, with short branches; from the L & Y, the Manchester–Bury and Liverpool–Southport lines; from the Midland, the short Lancaster–Morecambe–Heysham installation; and a nominal share in an electrified stretch of the London, Tilbury & Southend line as far as Upminster, although the electric trains were actually operated by the District Railway. All the LMS achieved in the inter-war years was some marginal extensions such as the Rickmansworth branch off the Watford line, plus electrification of the Wirral Railway (13 route miles) in 1938, and sharing with the LNER in electrification of the Manchester, South Junction, and Altrincham joint line (9 route miles) in 1931.

Again, the LMS made virtually no progress with the introduction of 20-ton wagons, which even the usually conservative GWR was promoting in South Wales. It was slow to mechanise its road collection and delivery services; its stud of horses, over 9,000 at the amalgamation, still amounted to over 8,000 at the beginning of the war period.

It was, perhaps, too concerned with defending its practices and policies with great energy, and not enough with critically re-examining them. The LMS public relations department was always high-powered, and great attention was paid to this activity by both Stamp and his successor, Wood.

Behind the front of modern business efficiency, there were shortcomings that affected morale. The cleanliness of engines and carriages fell far short of the standards of the old Midland or the Caledonian. Maintenance of passenger stations fell off in the search for economy and a certain dinginess spread. The huge, sprawling LMS, perhaps inevitably, could not give the 'feel' of a close-knit, well-supervised railway that some of its constituents had conveyed, and the loss of pride in its older buildings meant that when repairs or alterations were carried out, this was often done crudely, by engineering staff or contractors with no feeling for the original architectural concept. The LMS was in fact rather a Philistine in such matters.

The relentless search for economies by the Executive Research Office (a Stamp creation) was pursued in all aspects of paper consumption. The paper bought was cheapened, the printing made smaller and half-used sheets cut down for re-issue. In the end, only the President and Vice-Presidents could conduct their correspondence on paper whose quality suggested it had emanated from a great commercial undertaking with important customers; the other officers might have been writing from some poverty-stricken corner shop.

Stamp's great prestige, his quickness of mind and power of expression made him a formidable champion or witness. Had he survived, he would only have been 67 at the date of nation-alisation, and still in full vigour. He undoubtedly would have become Chairman of either the British Transport Commis-sion or the Railway Executive and the first few years of British Railways might have been much more firmly guided than actually was the case.

What Stamp lacked was first-hand experience – such as Sir Herbert Walker, for instance, fully possessed – of how the railway really operates at ground floor level. Stamp had to rely upon what he was told, upon statistics fed to him by his invaluable aide, W. V. Wood, and upon his own observations from his exalted position. He would not accept that these might be inadequate to reveal what was actually going on. He became very testy indeed with Frederick Smith, then chief transport executive of the Unilever group, who (himself an ex-railwayman) was arguing that the future of rail freight lay in train-load working, with distribution by road to and from a limited number of railhead centres. Prompted by his chief officers, Stamp quite angrily refused to accept this thesis or to agree that the railway's wagon-load freight services were at all unsatisfactory. Yet the Smith case became virtually the cornerstone of British Railways policy in the 1960s. What a pity that the railways did not accept it 30 years earlier when it might have stopped the downward slide of rail freight.

On the other hand, the LMS was more forward-looking than any other main line railway in setting up a Research Department and also a School of Transport at Derby. It was an energetic spokesman and proponent of the railway case for legislative changes, the so-called 'square deal' campaign of 1938–39, and it fought very hard during the anti-nationalisation campaign of 1946–47. It was a tough fighter all its life, sometimes hitting friends as well as enemies, and it did not perish without a struggle. Its two main legacies to British Railways were, however, both unfortunate – a central-ised form of management organisation that was abolished after six years' experience; and a mechanical engineering

36

department that tried to repeat the successes of 20 years earlier in building standard steam locomotives instead of anticipating the needs of the future.

CHAPTER 3

The Great Western Stands Firm

If a nation that has no history is happy, the railway that suffers no reorganisation is equally happy. From the melting-pot of the 1921 Act only the Great Western emerged virtually unchanged. It merely had to digest the Cambrian and the Midland & South Western Junction – both poverty-stricken lines – and a collection of South Wales coal railways and dock systems that, for the most part, had been prosperous until the war hit the coal export trade.

In the 1880s the Taff Vale had once paid a dividend of 17½ per cent on its ordinary stock, and 10 per cent had been common before 1914. In the post-war years until amalgamation it had been paying 4 per cent, which was not at all bad for those difficult times. It had also virtually unified its management with that of two other important South Wales lines, the Rhymney Railway and the Cardiff Railway, in the first world war. To some extent this foreshadowed and in the event may have simplified the amalgamations with the Great Western.

The Taff Vale's board room at Queen Street, Cardiff, reflected the company's prosperity; it would have been quite suitable to the dignity of the Great Western itself. The same could hardly be said of the Cambrian's relatively austere head offices in Oswestry. The contrast with the relatively prosperous South Wales lines was illustrated by the humiliating fact that, in the scheme of amalgamation, £100 of Cambrian Ordinary stock was exchanged for only £2.8s.6d. GWR Ordinary, not ranking for dividend before 1929.

So the Great Western was able to continue after 1923 very

much as it had done before the grouping. It digested the accretions without pain to itself, though the loss of identity and status was keenly felt by some of the staff who were taken over. The GWR was often alleged to be complacent – competitors called it 'God's Wonderful Railway' now that the cut-offs built in the first decade of the twentieth century had made it no longer the 'Great Way Round'. They joked that 'Paddington speaks only to Swindon, and Swindon speaks only to God', with perhaps a touch of envy.

Complacent or not, the GWR was a close-knit organisation with a strong family atmosphere. Even after amalgamation, the railway was of manageable size. The sudden expansion of the LMS, leading to struggles between equally balanced forces, had no parallel at Paddington, where differences might exist, but only between departments, not whole sections of the railway. Generally the tradition was one of unity and mutual support.

Apart from escaping the worst problems of grouping, the Great Western had a number of advantages. In the rural territory it served, and even in South Wales, railway employment generally compared favourably with alternative opportunities, so that there was keen competition to enter the railway service and staff of good quality were obtained automatically. There was a paternal, family feeling that manifested itself in staff welfare schemes supported by the directors. This in turn produced a favourable relationship with the travelling public; the GWR was held high in public esteem, even affection, over much of the territory it served.

Then, the railway had enjoyed both reasonable financial stability and a tradition of high-class engineering that had lasted without a break since the days of Brunel and Gooch. Its track and structures exemplified solid Victorian virtues, and it had an excellent safety record.

Above all, the Great Western had no real motive power problem other than that of rationalising and rebuilding the accretions to the locomotive stock from those minor railways that had been swept into the net. Under George Jackson Churchward, Swindon Works had equipped the Great Western with a fleet of excellent work-horses, fully adequate – with appropriate 'refreshment' through annual building programmes – to meet the needs of the Superintendent of the Line for motive power. Sir William Stanier, in a paper read in 1955 to the Newcomen Society, said that Churchward 'had a flair for selecting good engineering things' and was 'the most progressive locomotive engineer of his time'. In addition, he 'had a gift for selecting young men who were not only able, but were willing to carry out his ideas in actual practice. He selected Collett from the drawing office'. When Churchward retired in 1921 it had been clear that Collett would carry on and develop Churchward's ideas and not depart substantially from them. Hence the strong continuity in GWR locomotive policy, from 1902 (when Churchward became Locomotive, Carriage & Wagon Superintendent, later redesignated Chief Mechanical Engineer), right up to nationalisation in 1948.

From 1923 until nationalisation, the GWR had only two General Managers. Felix J. C. Pole (knighted in 1924) had taken up the post in 1921, when he was 45; he had started on the railway as a youth and worked his way up. He was hard-working and something of a perfectionist; the pace he set was not always to the liking of certain chief departmental officers accustomed to be left to run their departments as they thought fit.

The Great Western in fact had some of the defects of its virtues, namely conservatism and autocratic behaviour among its potentates. This could be a source either of strength or of weakness. It meant that the Chief Mechanical Engineer was something of a law unto himself, assuming that he had the support of the Locomotive Committee of the Board, to which he had direct access, although his formal recommendations required the General Manager's endorsement. The Chief Accountant had direct access to the Board, and the Superintendent of the Line, covering all train movement and

Railway heraldry: coats of arms or emblems of LMS (top left), *GWR* (top right), *LNER* (bottom left), *SR* (bottom right) (All National Railway Museum except GWR, British Rail)

Contrasts on the LMS. Below: *One of the superb Midland 12-wheeled dining carriages* (British Rail). Below right: *An ex-North London Railway four-wheeled brake van that survived into the 1930s* (L&GRP/David & Charles)

Above: *Part of the LMS inheritance: the LNWR signal gantry at Crewe South* (By courtesy of the National Railway Museum)

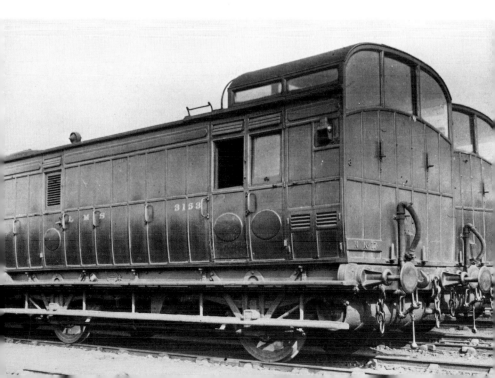

Above: *Scottish cleanliness and good design: Wemyss Bay station under the LMS but still very 'Caley' in character* (L&GRP/David & Charles)

Below: *Britain's first 4-6-0, the 'Jones Goods', still at work in LMS days* (L&GRP/David & Charles)

also the passenger commercial business, virtually managed the railway as he saw fit on a day-to-day basis.

After 1923, the Great Western pursued a policy of steady development of projects in the pipeline, though it had passed the major period of expansion that had seen the construction of the Severn Tunnel and the new direct routes to South Wales, to Birmingham and to the West of England. Steady progress rather than bold leaps forward was the aim.

It returned to the traditional chocolate and cream livery for its passenger carriages, which had been replaced before the first world war by a reddish-brown colour, much darker than the Midland's famous crimson lake.

On the locomotive side, just before the grouping, in 1922, Collett had produced the Castle class of 4–6–0, followed by the larger Kings of 1927 and the series of mixed-traffic Granges, Halls and Manors. All these really represented no more than variations and developments of Churchward's classic 4–6–0 designs, two-cylinder or four-cylinder, with the combination of taper boilers and long-travel valves, which not only produced steam in the volumes required but turned it efficiently and economically into tractive force.

If the locomotives formed a collection of close relatives, the same could hardly be said of passenger carriages. Here there was considerable variety; Swindon seemed unable to settle upon a standard design and keep it in production for any length of time. Main line trains might include 70ft long vehicles – the longest in Britain at the time, and only permissible because of the generous GWR loading gauge – and stock with recessed doors, made necessary because the clipper shape of the bodies had a maximum width of 9ft 7in at the waist. Other peculiarities included a fondness for deadlock, outside-only, door handles, which could be very stiff to turn but which the GWR for some reason considered safer than spring catches. The highlight of GWR carriage construction came early in the 1930s with the eight Ocean Special or Cunard saloons for the Plymouth Transatlantic boat trains, and all named after members of the Royal Family.

The operating methods of the Great Western were interesting. The system included some splendid racing grounds, relatively free from speed restrictions and severe gradients, such as the main lines from Paddington to Bristol, Birmingham and South Wales, but also difficult, severely graded routes such as Swindon–Gloucester, Taunton–Exeter and (above all) Exeter–Plymouth. There was a sharp contrast between the well-publicised prestige trains such as the Cornish Riviera Express with its non-stop run to Plymouth, 225½ miles in 4 hours 7 minutes, reduced at one time to 4 hours, and the later glamour trains, the Cheltenham Flier and the Bristolian, on the one hand, and the more leisurely timing of the generality of the services. The GWR tradition was one of gentle starts, followed by smooth running at reasonable speeds, depending on the character of the route, coupled with prolonged station stops which for some reason the timetable planners insisted upon providing. In fact, whenever a Great Western train pulled into a platform, this seemed a favourable opportunity for the train staff and the station staff to exchange views at length regarding the weather and the state of the crops in the neighbourhood! It was all very characteristic and not very exasperating to the passenger unless he was in a hurry and the train was already late. But on Sundays, when the Chief Engineer seemed to take possession of the entire system, it was anybody's guess when a train, diverted to unfamiliar routes and subject to lengthy sections of wrong line working executed at a very leisurely tempo, might be expected to arrive.

The few spectacular examples of very fast running did not really tax very severely the power of the available locomotives. The Cheltenham Flier, for instance, advertised as 'the fastest train in the world' for a time, was comparatively easily timed over the 35 miles of gradients between Gloucester and Swindon, and only 'flew' over the superbly straight, gently downhill stretch of 77¼ miles from Swindon to Paddington.

46

Perhaps it was assisted by the prevailing west wind, since no comparable run was made in the opposite direction! Much more exacting locomotive work was performed on the 'mountain' stretch between Exeter and Plymouth, where skilful firing and driving were essential.

One admirable feature of GWR operating practice, not extensively followed elsewhere between the wars, apart from the Southern Railway, was the adoption of clock-face departure times for the principal destinations served by down trains from Paddington. These regular timings were: 00.10 for Birmingham via High Wycombe; 00.15 for Bristol; 00.30 for the West of England; 00.45 for Oxford and the West Midland line; 00.55 for South Wales. Unfortunately, the timings in the up direction could not always be standardised, nor did the volume of traffic justify hourly departures to all these destinations on the true clock-face principle. And, as so often seems to happen, the standardised departures were progressively eroded, year by year, by minor alterations which, though justified individually, had the collective effect of largely destroying the pattern.

A special GWR feature was the number of slip carriages it continued to operate long after most other lines had abandoned, or virtually abandoned, the practice. It undoubtedly led to poor utilisation, for vehicles were confined to a single out-and-home circuit – and this applied also to the large number of through carriages or train portions divided en route. In some years the Cornish Riviera carried through coaches for nine destinations – Weymouth, Exeter, Minehead, Ilfracombe, Kingsbridge, Plymouth, Falmouth, St Ives and Penzance. On the down journey it slipped coaches at Westbury, Taunton and Exeter. Its number of destinations was only equalled by the Southern Railway's Atlantic Coast Express.

Another GWR peculiarity was the permanent painting on the side of certain non-passenger-carrying coaching vehicles not merely the stations between which they were to work, but

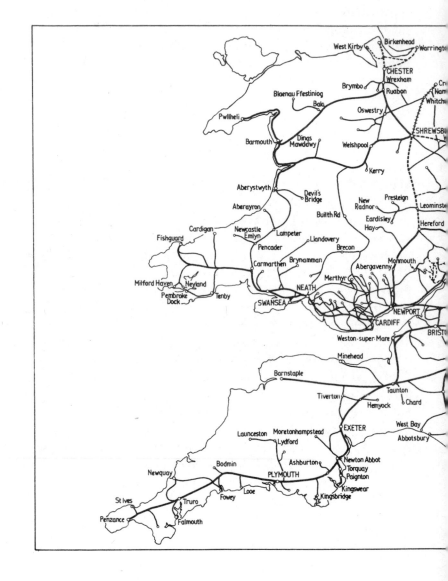

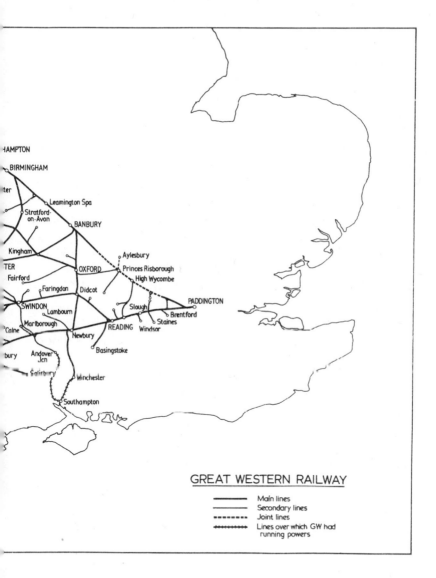

Map labels (as shown): HAMPTON, BIRMINGHAM, ter, Leamington Spa, Stratford-on-Avon, BANBURY, Kingham, Aylesbury, TER, OXFORD, Princes Risborough, Fairford, High Wycombe, Faringdon, Didcot, PADDINGTON, SWINDON, Lambourn, Slough, Brentford, Marlborough, Staines, Calne, READING, Windsor, Newbury, bury, Andover Jcn, Basingstoke, Salisbury, Winchester, Southampton

GREAT WESTERN RAILWAY

——— Main lines
——— Secondary lines
-------- Joint lines
+++++++ Lines over which GW had running powers

49

the actual times of the trains concerned, implying complete confidence in the continuity of the time-table for many years to come! The vehicles thus treated were newspaper vans, milk train brake vans, and some, if memory is correct, dedicated to sausages from Calne in Wiltshire, despatched to satisfy the cravings of aficionados in London.

The GWR had never operated Pullman cars – the concept of contracting out any part of the railway's operations was alien to the philosophy of Paddington and Swindon – until Felix Pole instituted the short-lived Torquay Pullman, as well as the use of Pullmans on the Plymouth ocean liner specials. This helped, incidentally, to exacerbate relations between Pole and his Chairman, Viscount Churchill, who was strongly opposed to Pullman services; it was probably one factor in the relatively early departure of Pole from the railway service to take up the Chairmanship of Associated Electrical Industries Ltd, in 1929.

Pole's successor was (Sir) James Milne, also a life-long GWR man but one who, despite being a strong personality, was able to maintain an easier relationship with the departmental officers, while at the same time enjoying full support from his Board.

The GWR's passenger operations were based upon a few show trains so far as speed was concerned, together with a rather slack, easy-going policy for the run-of-the-mill services. To a considerable extent this was also the case on the freight side. There were a few fast vacuum-braked through trains at creditable speeds, but otherwise everything was staged from one small yard to another, with a vast amount of trip working and remarshalling. In consequence, end-to-end journey times for individual wagons could be unpredictable, depending upon the congestion or otherwise at individual staging points. Freight train productivity, expressed as net ton-miles per total engine hour, was 418.7 in 1923, rising to 457.5, an increase of 9.3 per cent, in 1938. The LNER achieved an improvement of 19.8 per cent over the same period.

The leisurely, rather old-fashioned approach to freight operation was not seriously challenged before the second world war. But in the autumn of 1940 the United States authorities complained to the Ministry of War Transport in London that congestion in the South Wales ports managed by the GWR was delaying delivery of Lease-Lend supplies, and the Railway Executive Committee was instructed to improve the situation rapidly. The outstanding brain among railway operators at that time was C.M. Jenkin Jones, Divisional General Manager of the North Eastern Area of the LNER. He was despatched to South Wales with an urgent remit, and he quickly demanded changes and reforms which, although much resented by the GWR officers, had the desired effect.

Characteristically, however, there was also some striking GWR enterprise in freight transport before nationalisation. Then the GWR was endeavouring to rationalise collected and delivered traffic by establishing zonal centres in place of the small goods stations sited only a few miles apart, rebuilding and modernising a number of depots and concentrating all transhipment between rail wagons and road vehicles at major centres. More significantly still, where overall journeys were short, transfer from one zonal centre to another might be by trunk motor instead of by rail, where this could be quicker and cheaper. This system, using the road powers obtained by the railways in 1928, had in itself the germ of an integrated transport system; it was tragic that the compartmenting of activities under the Transport Act of 1947 put an end to this enterprising development.

This episode illustrates an aspect in which the GWR was well ahead of the other companies – the organisation of a Road Transport Department under a Chief Officer directly responsible to the General Manager. The GWR was particularly fortunate in possessing in F.C.A. Coventry a Superintendent of Road Transport who had many progressive ideas and who also enjoyed the status that enabled him to carry them out. An example of GWR enterprise had been the institution in 1929 of a combined road and rail service, with through tickets issued to passengers between Paddington and Cheltenham, the transfer between rail and road being effected at Oxford.

So far as structures were concerned, the GWR was perhaps in a favourable position compared with the other three grouped companies. Most of its more important stations were spacious, reasonably modern and well maintained. There were a few black spots still crying out for modernisation at the end of the GWR's existence, notably Oxford and Banbury. Taunton was a major reconstruction carried out during Pole's time. But Brunel's original, curious single-sided wooden stations at Reading, Slough, Taunton, Exeter and Gloucester had all been reconstructed at various times, since they could not be patched or adapted to meet modern traffic requirements.

It would therefore be wrong to over-emphasise the conservative side of GWR policy; the management at times were pioneers, even if the other companies did not follow the GWR lead. For instance, it tried hard to exploit the economies from larger coal wagons in place of the 10-ton and 12-ton boxes in practically universal use (except in the North Eastern Area of the LNER where 20-ton hoppers had long been standard). The GWR offered an inducement to traders to use 20-ton steel mineral wagons and persisted in this progressive policy despite only partial success.

Again, the GWR alone had what was described as automatic train control or, less ambitiously, as audible cab signalling, a precursor of BR's automatic warning system of today. Developed at Swindon, it was robust and simple in operation. A ramp between the running rails some 40ft long raised a shoe on a locomotive passing over it. It was situated close to a distant signal and was energised from an electric battery when the signal indicated clear. The raising of the shoe on the locomotive sounded a warning horn in the cab if the signal was at caution and the ramp dead – thus preserving the fail-safe principle – and the horn would blow until silenced by the driver. But if the signal was in the clear position and the ramp energised, the horn sequence would be cancelled and an electric bell sounded in the cab instead.

It had some weaknesses: being an electro-mechanical contact device, it relied upon accurate alignment between the ramp and the locomotive shoe. A locomotive bouncing on its springs or rolling badly *could* fail to receive an indication, but failures in practice were very few and the GWR's excellent safety record was certainly due in part to this useful safeguard.

The GWR was also a pioneer in the use of the diesel railcar, of which it operated a number on local and even cross-country services long before other railways had done more than toy with the idea. The Associated Equipment Company was owned by the London traffic combine – the Underground and London General Omnibus Group – until it had to be hived off under the London Passenger Transport Act of 1933. It had built buses for the LGOC, and it continued to do so for London Transport after 1933. Its works were situated at Southall and were rail-connected to the GWR main line.

The idea of a light railcar equipped with bus engines to replace steam push-and-pull trains took root, and the GWR had 18 diesel units in service by 1937, including a few equipped with a buffet for cross-country routes; a further batch brought the total to 34 by the early second world war years.

When nationalisation loomed ahead, the GWR, oddly enough, did not seem to enter into the anti-nationalisation campaign with quite the zest of the LMS. This was partly due to a certain incredulity among the majority of the officers at Paddington that anything so heinous could actually be about to happen, rather than to any resigned acceptance of the idea that a bunch of politicians could destroy the creation of Russell, Brunel, Gooch and Saunders. But, true to the GWR tradition of unorthodox thinking at unexpected times, it was whispered that the Chairman, Viscount Portal, might not be unwilling to sup with the Devil. And the General Manager, Sir James Milne, was actually offered the Chairmanship of the future Railway Executive, although he declined it, largely because he wanted to be able to retain certain outside directorships, and this the Minister would not concede.

So the GWR's demise, that had been averted in 1923, at last took place in 1948. But for years afterwards, under British Railways, the spirit and character of the GWR was kept alive at Paddington.

CHAPTER 4

The LNER: Three Railways or One?

One of the few actions which the London & North Eastern Railway shared with the London Midland & Scottish was an early contraction of its initials into a series that came smoothly off the tongue. 'LNER' soon replaced 'L&NER'; and after Eric Gill had later designed his famous Gill Sans type face for the railway's own use in all publicity material, the enclosure of the initials in a lozenge produced the 'totem' that was to become so widely used and recognised.

But if the totem suggested unity, the auspices at the railway's birth scarcely pointed in that direction. There was no single principle underlying the creation of the 'North Eastern, Eastern and East Scottish Group'. Fusion of the three companies that, by end-on junctions, had comprised the East Coast Route to Scotland well might be justified as a longitudinal amalgamation. But to tag on the Great North of Scotland was scarcely logical, since that railway had no physical connection with the North British, being separated by 38 miles of Caledonian (LMS) line from Kinnaber Junction to Aberdeen. Its main route was from Aberdeen to Inverness, yet it had to hand its trains over to the Highland (also LMS) at Elgin, 37 miles short of Inverness.

More important, the southern portion of the LNER consisted of three railways that radiated like the fingers of a hand from London – the 'Three Greats', Great Northern, Great Eastern and Great Central. Parliament had in fact as recently as 1909 forced the withdrawal of a Bill enabling these three companies to amalgamate, as being contrary to the public interest. Now they were being compulsorily thrown together.

It was true that the 'Three Greats' had voluntarily established a non-statutory pool of London cartage services, which
had effected some useful economies in van mileage, but otherwise there was not much in common between them. The
Great Eastern was a self-contained system serving East
Anglia as a virtual territorial monopoly, with heavy London
suburban traffic. Its main link with the Great Northern was
the GN & GE Joint Line from March to Doncaster, built to
carry Yorkshire coal to London. Otherwise it only touched
the GNR with its fingertips at Shepreth (near Cambridge), at
Huntingdon and at Peterborough.

As for the Great Central, the former 'railway flirt' had lost
its close association with the Great Northern over the King's
Cross to Manchester traffic via Retford and Sheffield when it
opened its own London Extension in 1899.

The Great Central had no regional monopoly anywhere; it
was competitive along practically every route, though not
with the Great Northern so much as the Midland. Throughout South Yorkshire and in parts of Derbyshire, Lancashire
and Cheshire the duplication of facilities by the GCR and the
MR was clearly excessive. Countless collieries and many
other industries, especially steel works, were connected to
both systems, and the consequent amount of trip working by
short trains to marshalling yards must have inflated costs
quite considerably. If real economies in working had been the
object of the grouping then it would have made better sense to
put the GCR and the Midland together. One would have felt
sorry for the able team of GCR officers that had been led by
dapper little Sir Sam Fay if they had come under the iron heel
of Derby!

Northward of the 'Three Greats' lay the territory of the
North Eastern – that well-managed, hitherto prosperous line
that traced its lineage back to the Stockton & Darlington and
the beginnings of railways. The NER was a monopoly to all
intents and purposes; the only challenge in recent years had
come from the struggling Hull & Barnsley, which the NER

was easily able to absorb even before the grouping, in 1922, and (to a lesser extent) from the Great Central after Immingham was built, across the Humber. The North Eastern bestrode the East Coast route, its hallmark the spacious and distinctive architecture of its great stations at York and Newcastle, so much more imposing than, say, Peterborough or Doncaster on the Great Northern. From the North Eastern was to come – it was expected – the sinews of war in the shape of revenues able to support the weaker brethren. From it also came an almost disproportionate amount of the management talent that was to shape the LNER.

The North Eastern also contributed to the new group its only electrified systems – the suburban network centred on Newcastle-upon-Tyne, 37 route-miles opened in 1904, and the freight-only route between Shildon and Newport, 18 route-miles, opened in 1915.

Further north still, the North British, although a competitor of the Caledonian for important traffics, did not enjoy the 'Caley's' financial strength and confident management. It had a tradition of struggle behind it, and the need for economy dominated its Board. As for the little 'Great' North of Scotland, it had outlived a rather discreditable past and was now a collection of lines, mainly serving agriculture and the fishing industry, well managed in an unostentatious way.

This very heterogeneous collection of railways had to be welded together somehow. From the outset, thinking about this problem was more relaxed and liberal than on the LMS. William Whitelaw, a public figure in Scotland with industrial interests, a successful Chairman of the North British Railway, was elected LNER Chairman, taking over with general acceptance a role that might conceivably have gone to Lord Knaresborough of the NER, Lord Faringdon of the GCR or Sir Frederick Banbury of the GNR.

The establishment of the LNER as what its critics called a federation of railways, rather than a single railway, was the result of much thought and deliberate decision, and not just the result of indecisive power struggles. Well before the appointed day of 1 January 1923, the Chairman-elect, William Whitelaw, was meeting an Organisation Committee of future LNER Directors and it was firmly decided to decentralise management as far as possible. This suited the Chairman's own temperament; he had come from two relatively small systems, the Highland and the North British, and had no inclination to see the big battalions obliterate the characteristics of their smaller brethren.

Another factor (though its full impact was only felt later on) was the shortage of funds for investment. This meant that far-reaching schemes of standardisation, designed ultimately to yield economies but initially requiring substantial investment outlays, were out of the question. So there was a general willingness to perpetuate existing practices unless these were actually detrimental to the interests of the group.

The new Chairman, although inclined to scrutinise very carefully indeed any proposals involving expenditure, had nothing else in common with the autocratic Richard Moon of the LNWR. He thoroughly enjoyed his railway activities; nothing pleased him better than a trip on the footplate or a day out inspecting the line in an officer's saloon. But at the same time he fully respected the managerial functions of his Chief General Manager and forbore to trespass on management's proper responsibilities.

To head the management, it was decided that the best choice was obvious. The LNER was thereby spared the difficulties which beset the LMS in finding a chief executive. Certainly there were strong personalities around; but Sir Sam Fay of the GCR had reached retiring age and Sir Henry Thornton, the dynamic American-born General Manager of the GER, had been tempted away to Canada by the offer of the Presidency of the Canadian National Railways – something he probably lived to regret. James Calder of the North British and C. H. Dent of the GNR both lacked the ambition to be serious contenders; and so it was arranged quite

58

amicably that the outstanding figure among the younger managers, Ralph Lewis Wedgwood, Deputy General Manager of the NER, should succeed to the General Managership of that railway at the beginning of 1922 to groom him for the future Chief General Managership of the new group. This was facilitated by the generous co-operation of the previous incumbent, Sir Alexander Kaye Butterworth, a very able and active 67-year-old, who had been himself considered as a possible Chief General Manager or even Chairman of the new group, but who preferred to ensure Wedgwood's future succession. It was all very civilised.

The Board and Wedgwood saw eye to eye from the outset about the need to avoid setting up a centralised 'monolith', managed from London. There was even discussion of the possibility of making York the headquarters. Very soon the Board's Organisation Committee had determined upon three main Areas – Southern, North Eastern and Scottish – with for the time being a sub-division of Scotland, more notional than practical, into a Northern and a Southern Scottish Area. It is interesting that no lip-service whatever was paid to any theory that the Areas should be roughly equal in size – the contrast between the Southern, comprising the 'Three Greats', and the Northern Scottish, consisting of no more than the GNSR, was striking. Within a few years the Northern Scottish Area disappeared and the LNER settled down in a sort of holy trinity of management – its critics called it the régime of three emperors, but it worked surprisingly well and the struggles between North Western and Midland influences on the LMS had no parallel on the LNER.

It was true that the North Eastern was something of a big brother, even though the Southern Area was much bigger than the North Eastern Area. But the NER had been in the league of top-notch pre-grouping companies, ranking with the LNWR, the GWR and the Midland; the 'Three Greats' had only enjoyed membership of the second grade. The York

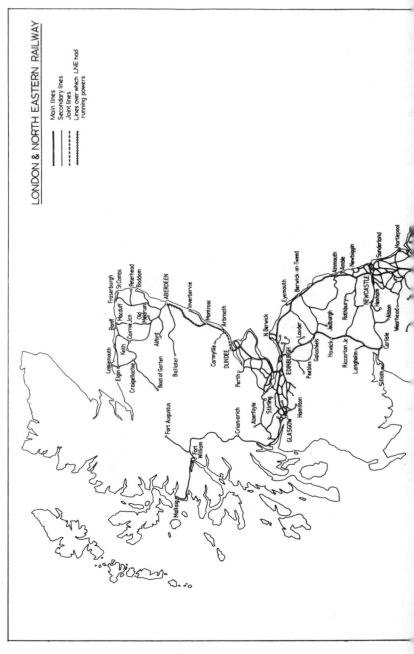

LONDON & NORTH EASTERN RAILWAY

Main lines
Secondary lines
Joint lines
Lines over which LNE had
running powers

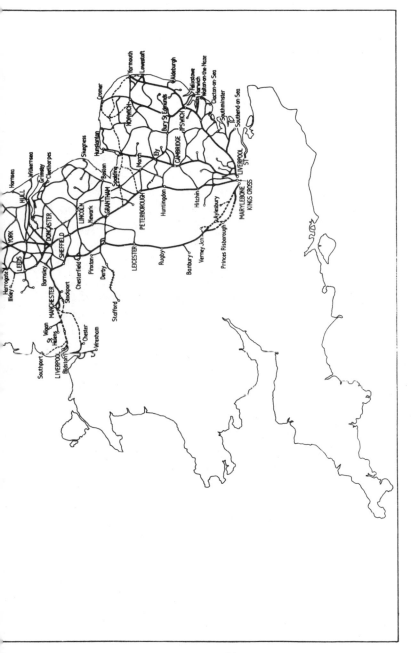

offices retained their old dignity; visitors from the south were made to feel that, whatever the formal organisation, here was the real heart of the LNER.

After about 1928 the organisation had stabilised, with the Areas in, very roughly, a 5–3–2 weighting, which was not without advantages. A young manager could cut his teeth in a departmental job in Edinburgh, and move on promotion to the equivalent post, first at York and eventually at Liverpool Street, where the Southern Area Divisional General Manager held court in the old GER General Offices. The Southern Area had in fact inherited three large London termini with former company headquarters adjacent, not to mention its interest in Fenchurch Street. The LNER board room, Chairman's and Secretary's offices were put into Marylebone; King's Cross housed the Chief General Manager; Liverpool Street became the Southern Area headquarters.

This, on paper, very loose-knit organisation, worked pretty well on the whole. Outside critics said it was irrational to have not one but three Goods Managers, three Passenger Managers and no less than four Superintendents (the Southern Area was split for operating purposes between a Western Section (ex-GN and ex-GC) and an Eastern Section (ex-GE). Certainly a departmental committee structure had to be set up to agree policies and practices that were not purely domestic to one Area. But, if less well paid, management felt more relaxed and freer to express opinions and to make suggestions to superiors, than was the case on the LMS. In fact, debate and diversity of views were sometimes encouraged, as leading to the best solutions.

Shortage of money and not shortage of ideas was the LNER's problem. The hope that the North Eastern Area would be able to support financially the weaker brethren, both to the north and to the south, was torpedoed by the long depression in coal mining, iron and steel, and shipbuilding, even before the general economic blizzard struck in 1930–1. Even so, with a good deal of make-do and mend, the LNER was able to show enterprise in many directions and was always looking for attractive goods to put in its shop window, without having to dig too heavily into its pocket. One need only recall the Gresley Pacifics, the non-stop London–Edinburgh runs, the Pullman services, the East Anglian and the Hook Continental, and above all the advent of the High Speed Trains in 1935 (antedating BR's use of the title by 40 years!). But the LNER was in fact essentially a freight railway; in 1924, a year after grouping, 61 per cent of its traffic receipts came from goods traffic, compared with 58 per cent on the LMS, 56 per cent on the GWR and only 26 per cent on the SR. So, although the long-standing East Coast Conference, established well before the first world war between the GNR, NER and NBR to foster Anglo-Scottish traffic, was very much concerned with express passenger services from King's Cross to Edinburgh and Aberdeen, it also paid attention to fast braked goods trains, and the East Coast Conference had its own cartage in Edinburgh and Glasgow to speed up door-to-door services. Robert Bell, for long Assistant General Manager of the LNER, and himself an old North Eastern man, commented though that 'the NE often found the GN slow in fostering traffic across the Border Perhaps its Board took more pride in its Leeds and King's Cross services'. Certainly the West Riding expresses, even more than the Anglo-Scottish services, were the Great Northern's crack trains, stimulated no doubt by the keen competition from the Midland.

Such money as was available had therefore to be channelled into the freight business as well as the more glamorous express passenger trains – and into docks and steamships, all clamouring for investment. March (Whitemoor) was the first freight marshalling yard in this country to be equipped with retarders, and for many years it was something of a showpiece in mechanised wagon sorting.

A good example of the LNER's ability to obtain public esteem quite inexpensively was the commissioning of the special Gill Sans type face widely used in the Company's printing and display advertising, which was an important element in promoting a 'corporate identity' for the railway. This elegant lettering – which had some affinities with the Johnston type face used by the Underground – combined well with the pictorial component in LNER posters, of which many striking ones were commissioned from different artists, rivalling the famous series painted for the LMS by Norman Wilkinson, RA.

The Board and the Chief General Manager were fortunate in having in Herbert Nigel Gresley, later Sir Nigel, a Chief Mechanical Engineer who was able to live with the financial limitations imposed on his department and at the same time to show the company's flag by designing locomotives that, even if they could not be standardised and produced in very large numbers, were technically striking and always caught the public's attention. Gresley certainly enjoyed the limelight but he was never self-satisfied or narrow-minded. He built several batches of locomotives to pre-grouping designs of past CMEs, because they happened to be admirably suited to the demands of the operating department, where a lesser man might have insisted upon redesigning them himself. Yet Gresley had his less successful designs such as the 4–4–0 Hunt class, and his huge P2 2–8–2 engines for the Edinburgh–Aberdeen route were not entirely successful as eight-coupled machines and were later rebuilt as Pacifics. He was neither over-obstinate nor a prima donna like some other CMEs, and his relationship with Wedgwood was one of cordial mutual respect.

The relatively loose rein on which the Areas were controlled from headquarters meant that differences in working practices persisted for many years after amalgamation. In consequence, many good features of the constituent companies were not submerged in dull uniformity. The Great Eastern for instance maintained its tradition, dating back to the days of its Chairman known as 'Punctuality Parkes', of short station stops and smart working. The Great Central kept alive the competitive drive of Sam Fay's time that had inspired its policy of fast if lightly loaded trains with excellent refreshment facilities. The Great Northern retained the excellence of its permanent way that gave such smooth running.

Spreading the butter, in the shape of investment resources, very thinly on the bread was an exercise in which the LNER became, through necessity, very proficient. It was also skilled at extracting the maximum favourable publicity from service improvements that did not involve heavy capital expenditure. For example, the much-advertised non-stop running of the Flying Scotsman between London and Edinburgh cost little more than the provision of a handful of corridor tenders enabling the enginemen to be changed at the half-way point without stopping the train. Extensive use was made of arrangements with the Pullman Car Company that obviated the need for extensive investment in new restaurant cars. On the Great Eastern section, Pullman day trips to various resorts, collectively described as Eastern Belle services, were provided by a train set also used on occasions for race specials to Newmarket. Even the famous streamliners – the High Speed Trains inaugurated in 1935 with the Silver Jubilee – that set new standards in travel between London and the North-East, the West Riding, and the Scottish capital, did not involve very high investment. Streamlining the locomotives was not a costly item and the whole service was provided with a handful of new train sets. Incidentally, expenditure on special signalling such as BR have become involved in providing for the Advanced Passenger Train 40 years later, was avoided simply by operating the High Speed Trains under double block working, that is with two block sections clear, thus ensuring a safety margin or additional over-run to compensate for the extra braking distance required – an inexpensive expedient, though one which could involve some adverse effects upon the timetabling and running of ordinary trains.

If the LNER was rather sprawling and diversified, it was

very efficient in special sectors of its operations. The Harwich (Parkeston Quay) Continental services were popular. The ships were well-found and comfortable and the connecting train between London and Harwich was almost luxurious – spotlessly maintained, with an excellent Pullman (later restaurant car) service. The Great Eastern had always enjoyed, like the Midland, a high standard of catering both in its restaurant cars and, more especially, at the Great Eastern Hotel at Liverpool Street.

The LNER hotels presented an interesting contrast with those of the LMS. Apart perhaps from the Great Eastern (London), the North British (Edinburgh) and the Royal Station Hotel (York), they tended to be rather less pretentious but to offer more solid bourgeois comfort and perhaps a friendlier atmosphere. One may contrast the LNER's Great Northern Hotels in London, in Leeds and in Bradford, the North British in Glasgow, or the Royal Victoria in Sheffield, with the LMS Midland in Manchester, Midland Adelphi in Liverpool, Queen's in Leeds or the Central Station in Glasgow, and by no means altogether to the disadvantage of the smaller, homelier LNER establishments.

A typical example of LNER enterprise was the 'Beer Trains' as the undergraduates quickly christened them – they were officially named 'Garden Cities and Cambridge Buffet Expresses' – comprising short, smartly timed trains linking King's Cross with the two Garden Cities of Welwyn and Letchworth and with Cambridge. Originally powered by the small-boilered Atlantics dating back to 1900, they were later entrusted to the large-boilered Atlantics and had considerable appeal for the connoisseurs of both fast trains and beer!

Another unique venture, again avoiding new investment but using resources already available, was the Northern Belle touring train which offered almost a week's rail cruising in picturesque country around Scotland. Passengers passed the nights in sleeping cars and most meals were served in restaurant cars, but daytime travel by rail was varied with road excursions and some hotel meals.

Despite all this ingenuity and the good impression created by such examples of enterprise, the LNER was always hampered by its weak financial position. In its best years, 1923 and 1929, its traffic receipts were between £58.8 million and £55.6 million; but the effects of the depression were such that in 1932 they had fallen to £42.7 million, enforcing drastic economies. The consequence was the inability to carry through many schemes of improvement which cried out for execution. Abandonment of the North Eastern Railway's scheme for main line electrification between York and New-castle was perhaps a pity but steam performance over this section of line was good. The failure to electrify the Great Eastern suburban services from Liverpool Street, though, was serious; it had been staved off under the GER by two rather shaky expedients. First, James Holden's Decapod 0–10–0 tank engine of 1902/3 had demonstrated an ability to accel-erate a 300-ton train from rest to 30 mph in 30 seconds. This was supposed to show that steam could match the perform-ance of electricity, though once the demonstration was over the civil engineers quietly put the stopper on any multiplica-tion of Decapods and the prototype retired, rebuilt as a 0–8–0 tender locomotive, to freight work.

The second expedient had been what a journalist termed 'The Last Word in Steam-operated Suburban Services' – the so-called 'Jazz Service' between Liverpool Street, Enfield and Chingford. Devised by Fred Russell, a mechanical engineer with (like Cecil Paget) a flair for operating who in fact became Superintendent of Operations, it was based on inten-sive utilisation and what nowadays might be termed an Orga-nisation and Method study of this particular train service. Its effect was to speed up the service and offer more seats to passengers without building a single new locomotive or car-riage. Impressive as a demonstration of what can be done with old assets by intensive planning and split-second timing, it was still no final answer to the real need to modernise and electrify these services, which was not carried through until well after nationalisation.

The LNER's inability to fund such necessary projects was only relieved by the Government scheme to relieve unemployment through financing public works. The Railway Finance Corporation and London Electric Transport Finance Corporation loans at minimum rates of interest at last allowed the LNER to undertake some cherished electrification schemes. Hitherto it was merely shared with the LMS in the short Manchester South Junction & Altrincham suburban electrification; now it was decided to electrify some of the Great Eastern suburban lines – not, this time, those to Enfield and Chingford but the Ilford and Shenfield section of the main line where complaints of overcrowding and delays were serious. In addition, the heavy coal traffic across the Pennines by the GCR Woodhead Tunnel route was to be electrified. Other GER suburban routes were to be handed over to London Transport for the Central Line tube to be extended over them. None of these works was completed when the second world war broke out and they had to be suspended.

The last decade of the LNER was different from the earlier period in several ways. Both the Chairman and Chief General Manager retired. Whitelaw was replaced by Sir Ronald Matthews, a Sheffield industrialist of considerable charm and very quick wit, but one who, with his industrial background, was more inclined to participate in what his predecessor might have considered purely managerial decision-making. Sir Ralph Wedgwood was followed by C.H. (Sir Charles) Newton, a large and kindly man and a capable former Chief Accountant, but who did not share the intellectual power of Wedgwood. Gresley, now Sir Nigel, died in harness relatively early in the war, in 1941, and his policies were considerably modified by his successor, Edward Thompson – a case of a Darlington man following a Doncaster man and paying off some old scores!

Like all the railways during the war the LNER had to cope

Above: *Probably the most luxurious inner suburban electric stock ever built; one of the ex-LNWR sets at Addison Road on the Willesden Junction–Earl's Court service* (L&GRP/David & Charles)

Below: *In contrast the ex-Midland electrics on the Lancaster–Morecambe–Heysham line had wooden seats in the third class* (By courtesy of the National Railway Museum, York)

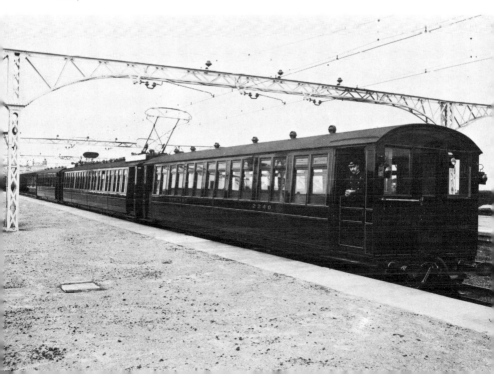

Above: *A demonstration of 'telescoping': the Leighton Buzzard accident on the LMS, 22 March 1931* (Crown copyright, National Railway Museum)

Below: *John Shearman's ingenious 'Ro-Railer' of 1931 changing wheels* (L&GRP/ David & Charles)

as best it could with heavy new demands but very few new resources; but after the war it had great plans for the future – a £50 million programme of investment which was more than twice the company's total capital expenditure between 1923 and 1938. It had participated fully in the re-think about the railways' role in the post-war world, ideas which were largely to be scrapped under nationalisation. The Board also approved a diesel traction project for the whole of the East Coast Main Line services, which too was scrapped on nationalisation.

The real legacy of the LNER to British Railways, however, was management talent. Robert Bell, Wedgwood's dour Scots Assistant General Manager, had consistently supervised the recruitment, the training and the career development of young managers in a way that yielded great benefit to the company. The North Eastern Railway had pioneered a traffic apprenticeship scheme under which three years' intensive training in the main branches of railway work was given to selected university graduates entering railway service, together with a similar number of specially promising young men from the clerical grades. After training, this development was continued by careful job rotation personally planned by Robert Bell in close consultation with the Area Managers.

Such intense control of career development offset, and more than offset, the sad fact that the LNER felt unable to pay most of its managers salaries that matched those common on the other great companies. The wind was somewhat tempered to those shorn lambs, who might consider themselves fortunate to receive a £25 pa advance in salary, by the fact that the LNER was sometimes more generous in extending travel privileges to junior officers than were some other lines.

In the event, it was striking in the years following nationalisation how many former LNER men emerged as the best natural candidates for senior management posts. It was a tribute to a great company tradition, and to Robert Bell.

CHAPTER 5
The Southern Emerges

Since nationalisation the Southern Region of British Railways seems to have had more than its share of problems and also perhaps more than its share of public criticism. It is therefore interesting to recall that its predecessor, the Southern Railway, had a record of steady progress and increasing public favour almost continuously throughout its life. There were those in the management of the other companies who sneered that the Southern was only a tramway. The Chairman of the LNER, Sir Ronald Matthews, once snorted 'The Southern have no problems'. The fact is, that the Southern solved its problems in a practical way as they emerged, perhaps not always finding the ideal solution but always a realistic one.

Two factors assisted the Southern's steady rise both in efficiency and public esteem. One was that it started from a rather low level of popularity on the South Eastern side in particular, so that any real improvement would be welcomed by the public. The second was the continuity in leadership, and strong leadership also given by Sir Herbert Walker, General Manager almost from the inception until 1937, whose influence continued to be felt by his appointment – after a short pause – as a director, right until nationalisation.

The new group comprised only three major constituents – the London & South Western, the London, Brighton & South Coast and the South Eastern & Chatham. It was a peculiarity of the last-named that, although it was a statutory body managing a railway undertaking, it did so on behalf of the two companies, formerly competitors – the South Eastern Railway and the London, Chatham & Dover Railway – which continued in existence as financial entities still administering some activities excluded from the SECR joint account.

The minor components comprised the Isle of Wight railway companies and the narrow-gauge Lynton & Barnstaple line, as well as various odds and ends.

Competition between the three main constituents, radiating like the fingers of a hand from London, in their last independent years had not been very keen. At such frontier towns as Portsmouth and Hastings, working arrangements existed that had removed its impact – and also perhaps its spur to efficiency. And joint lines (such as the Oxted route) and running powers (such as the SER and the LSWR possessed over sections of each other's lines between Guildford and Reading) were familiar. Part of the South Eastern former main line to Dover had been owned by the Brighton, and part of the Brighton's main line between London Bridge and Redhill by the South Eastern – a recipe for friction that largely disappeared when the South Eastern built its direct line from St John's to Tonbridge in 1868, and still more when the direct Quarry line was opened by the Brighton in 1900.

The Brighton and the SECR also had neighbouring head offices at London Bridge. In short, the three Southern constituents knew each other well, and even if there was an occasional dispute it was like a disagreement within the family – something very different from, for instance, the traditional deep-seated enmity between the 'Caley' and the 'Sou-West' in Scotland.

The SECR had moreover by 1923 long outgrown the bitter rivalry between the SER and the LCDR that had only been ended by the creation of the single system under its statutory Managing Committee in 1899. It had – rather like the Great Central – more ideas than money with which to carry them out. The first world war had left it somewhat exhausted in physical terms, but it was energetically considering the electrification – long overdue – of its London suburban services. Its operating techniques, given the complexity of its routes, were quite advanced at such locations as Borough Market

73

Junction where a huge traffic was handled in the peak hours over a complex series of points and crossings. But the steam suburban services were unpopular because of elderly rolling stock, overcrowding, and unpunctuality.

The LBSC had the advantage of an electrified suburban network which needed extension to be fully comprehensive. It had a few crack trains, such as the Southern Belle Pullman to Brighton, but the pace of most of its services was leisurely; again, a good deal of its passenger rolling stock was rather antiquated.

The strongest partner was certainly the LSWR which was not merely a commuter railway but a major trunk line stretching from London to Cornwall, with a great port in Southampton, and a not inconsiderable freight traffic. It had even run sleeping cars on Plymouth ocean liner expresses for a few years of hectic competition with the Great Western. It handled a large amount of traffic from Waterloo, the terminus that had been some 30 years in reconstruction before, in 1922, it was officially declared complete by Queen Mary. But, despite a few bright spots of express train performance, the LSWR was not really a fast line and it owned a good deal of obsolescent rolling stock.

Still, under Walker's energetic guidance, the LSWR had already made a start with suburban electrification, rather later than the Brighton and on a different system. Whereas the latter used alternating current at 6,600 volts with overhead wire current collection, the LSWR had adopted direct current at 660 volts with third rail collection.

At the beginning of the Southern Railway there were hints of power struggles to decide which of the three major constituent companies was to be top dog, and also which system of electrification was to be adopted for future extension.

Management styles were interestingly varied. Both on the LSWR and the LBSCR, promotion to top posts could be gained by those who had worked their way up from the lower grades, and who enjoyed no special educational advantages.

But the SECR was rather a 'gentlemanly' railway, somewhat akin to the LNWR, with its trainees and its sprinkling of university graduates. Perhaps this was not altogether surprising, since the intellectual demands created by its operating and financial problems exceeded those of the other two partners. Even so, on all three railways had been notable importations to some senior posts. On the LSWR they included the General Manager, the Secretary, the Solicitor, the Locomotive Superintendent, the Carriage & Wagon Superintendent, and the Chief Engineer; on the LBSC the General Manager, the Solicitor, the Goods Manager, the Carriage & Wagon Superintendent; and on the SECR the General Manager, the Resident Engineer, the Chief Mechanical Engineer, and the Goods Manager.

For nearly a year the new Southern Railway Board shirked the issue of management control. At the outset it appointed all *three* general managers of the major constituents as joint general managers of the Southern. It was an impossible situation and Sir Herbert Walker found it intolerable. He was the youngest of the three but undoubtedly the most able, and moreover he had acted as Chairman of the wartime Railway Executive Committee of general managers. He was an outstanding railwayman in every way.

Eventually the SR Board accepted the inevitable and arranged for Sir William Forbes from the SECR and Sir Percy Tempest from the LBSCR to retire, leaving Walker in sole charge as from 1 January 1924. So began a memorable period of over 13 years' leadership which in effect transformed the Southern.

An initial measure was the creation of an operating organisation based upon Divisions that in the London suburban area to some extent ignored former company boundaries. The Divisions were: London (East); London (West); Eastern (Dover); Southern (Brighton); Central (Southampton); and Western (Exeter). This pattern, however, was modified a few years later, all the ex-SECR lines falling under the London

(East) Division and the ex-LBSCR lines under a new London (Central) Division. Only the ex-LSWR lines retained geographical decentralisation, with offices at Southampton and Exeter.

A new commercial organisation followed, and led to the merging of the headquarters operating and commercial departments under the control of a Chief Traffic Manager, an outstanding railwayman in whom Walker placed the greatest trust, E. C. Cox.

Apart from organisational questions, the most pressing problem confronting Walker was that of electrification of the steam-operated London suburban services. Here the clash of systems created a serious problem. The London, Brighton & South Coast company had, for reasons that satisfied them and on the advice of a leading consulting electrical engineer, chosen the overhead a.c. system. The extra power that could be drawn at such a high voltage, when required, was particularly relevant in view of the company's intention to electrify the main line to Brighton. Another was the absence of interference with permanent way maintenance, such as that imposed by the third rail. Yet another was the much wider spacing of sub-stations, with consequent saving in distribution costs.

On the other hand the cost of the overhead supports for the catenary system of the conductor wire was considerable. There was interference in places with visibility of signals which needed to be re-sited, and, in practice, the motors installed by the LBSC in its a.c. suburban train sets were of rather low power so that acceleration was poor.

Walker had persuaded the LSWR Board to adopt direct current with third rail collection for the LSWR's first electrification schemes in 1915 and 1916, covering various inner suburban routes, including Shepperton and Hampton Court branches, because its simplicity and economy in first cost appealed to him. Its drawbacks were the limits upon the amount of current that could be taken in a single section of line, the much closer spacing of sub-stations, the problem of icing of the conductor rail in winter, interference with permanent way maintenance, and some increased risk to persons on the track whether there legitimately or otherwise.

Walker swung the SR Board to his point of view and in the short term he was undoubtedly right. With the d.c. system the huge programme of inner suburban electrification was carried out more quickly and cheaply than if overhead current collection had been employed. But when electrification extended to the coastal towns of Brighton, Eastbourne, Hastings, and Portsmouth, the balance probably swung the other way. Certainly the post-nationalisation extensions to Dover and Bournemouth, many engineers feel, would have been better carried out with a.c. overhead current supply.

Once started, the rolling programme of electrification moved steadily onward. In 1925 however an extension of the LBSCR overhead system, planned some time before, took place with continuation of electrification of the lines from Balham to Coulsdon, and between Selhurst and Sutton. Walker accepted that these schemes had to be completed even though his main aim was standardisation of the third rail. Three months after these last LBSCR projects were carried out, a major collection of lines on both the South Western and South Eastern Divisions was electrified, taking the third rail from Waterloo to Guildford and Dorking, and from Victoria and Holborn Viaduct to Orpington and Crystal Palace.

The South Eastern lines began to be electrified in 1926, from Charing Cross and Cannon Street to Orpington, Bromley North and Addiscombe. In the same year came the North Kent, Bexleyheath and Dartford lines. Two years later came the lines from London Bridge to Tattenham Corner and Caterham, Sydenham and Crystal Palace; and now the Brighton line had the third rail laid to Coulsdon North and over the South London line between Victoria and London Bridge. The next year the overhead system on the Brighton was finally abandoned and conversion to d.c. was complete.

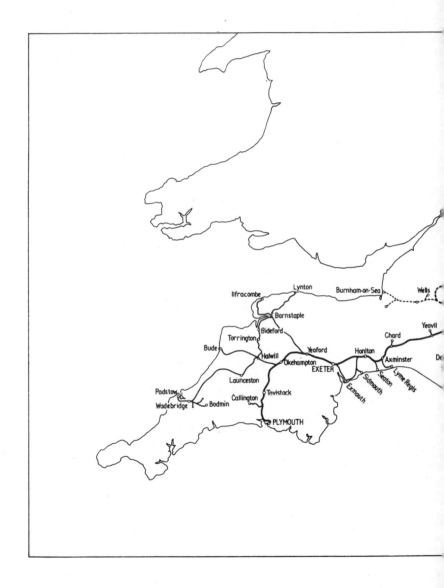

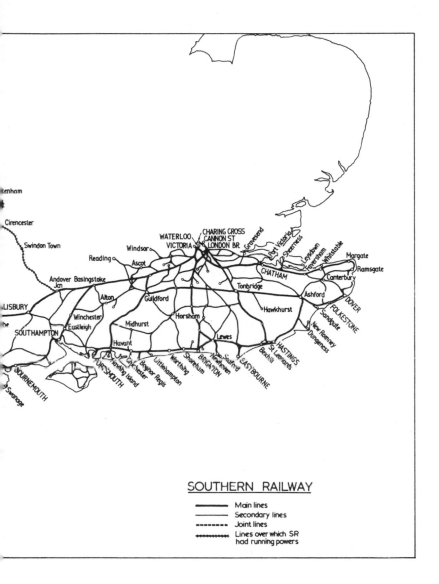

Cirencester

Swindon Town

Reading

Andover Basingstoke
Jcn

LISBURY

Alton

Winchester

Eastleigh

SOUTHAMPTON

Havant

BOURNEMOUTH

Swanage

Windsor

Ascot

Guildford

Midhurst

Hayling Island

PORTSMOUTH

Chichester

Bognor Regis

Littlehampton

Worthing

Shoreham

BRIGHTON

WATERLOO
VICTORIA

CHARING CROSS
CANNON ST
LONDON BR.

Horsham

Lewes

Newhaven

Seaford

Gravesend

Port Victoria

Sheerness

Loydown

Faversham

Whitstable

Margate

Ramsgate

CHATHAM

Tonbridge

Ashford

Canterbury

Hawkhurst

EASTBOURNE

HASTINGS

St Leonards

Bexhill

DOVER

FOLKESTONE

Sandgate

New Romney

Dungeness

SOUTHERN RAILWAY

————	Main lines
——	Secondary lines
- - - - -	Joint lines
+++++++	Lines over which SR had running powers

In 1930 the third rail reached Gravesend and Windsor, Redhill, Reigate and Three Bridges, while in 1933 the first real main line – that to Brighton and Worthing – was electrified. By this time the policy had become one of general electrification wherever traffic density could justify the outlay, so that Eastbourne and Hastings, Portsmouth (by two routes) and Reading were all reached by Southern Electric before Walker retired in 1937.

One feature of the Walker policy was standard running times outside the peak hours, on the clock-face principle. The hour was the basis for long-distance trains, with regular-interval departures at 30, 20 or 15 minutes for the denser services. 'To Brighton on the hour, in the hour, at the hour' was one of his precepts which was long remembered. Apart from the good utilisation of rolling stock which this promoted, and the convenience to passengers of often being able to dispense with timetables, it facilitated bus and rail connections at many country centres. Bus timetables are also based, as a rule, on the hourly pattern, subdivided as appropriate, so that Southern trains and buses could easily connect. These connections were of course facilitated by the greatly improved train punctuality which electrification brought with it.

This achievement of electrification not merely distinguishes the Southern from the other main lines but differs significantly from the principal electrification schemes on various Regions since nationalisation. First, it was essentially a rolling programme, under which the planning teams could be kept together and, one task completed, could move smoothly on to the next. This applied to main contractors as well as to railway staff. The benefits were great, in avoiding the loss of momentum and the costly delays in regaining it which have characterised Government 'stop-go' policies for railway investment ever since the second world war.

Walker persuaded the Southern Board that electrification was not merely a means of effecting economies in working but was actually a potent factor in stimulating traffic. This is so widely accepted today and graphically described as the 'sparks effect', that one forgets what a narrow, almost grudging view of electrification was taken by many railway officers between the wars, as something only justifiable in special circumstances. The Government's own Weir Committee on Main Line Electrification, which reported in 1931, had also concentrated attention upon cost reductions and envisaged only a very modest return on the outlays for two schemes examined.

Walker overcame this contemporary lack of enthusiasm for electrification by several means. First, he was an excellent judge of financial propositions. Next, he insisted upon eliminating any frills that were not essential to the electrification project itself, and exercised a strict control over estimating, progress checking and finally the monitoring of results. Lastly, he demonstrated that increased traffic followed the third rail everywhere.

Like all railways, the Southern in these years did not find capital-raising very easy. Walker was able to draw substantially upon internal sources of finance – renewal funds in particular – to meet much of the cost of electrification and this minimised expenditure from capital account. It was assisted by his policy of keeping electrification distinct from general modernisation of the line such as the London Midland Region of BR undertook with electrification from London to Birmingham, Liverpool and Manchester in the 1960s. Second-hand but serviceable carriage bodies from steam stock were mounted on new underframes and bogies. Stations had their platforms lengthened but were not reconstructed and indeed on the newly electrified lines many stations continued to be lit by gas! Semaphore signalling was not replaced merely in consequence of electrification; extensive conversion to multiple-aspect colour-light signalling *did* take place, but it had to be justified on its own merits as a separate project.

Confidence in the accuracy of Walker's financial judgment grew as traffic returns flowed in from each completed project.

The only time that the Board turned him down was over the proposal to electrify to Hastings via Tunbridge Wells. With hindsight, one can see that the Board's overcaution here was a mistake; had the scheme been carried out at 1937/38 prices it would almost certainly have paid and would have given a much better service than the diesel-electric multiple-unit trains later introduced by British Railways.

The Southern, when Walker retired from the General Managership, was still an extensive user of steam locomotives. The Kent Coast trains to Margate and Ramsgate, and to Folkestone and Dover, including the Continental boat trains, the Southampton, Bournemouth and Weymouth expresses, and the West of England expresses were all steam hauled. All freight was of course steam-operated. So were many cross-country lines and branches, even within what might be considered 'electric' territory.

The Southern, despite its down-to-earth approach and its heavy commitment to the London commuter traffic, never forgot that it was also a trunk line. There was a touch of real glamour about the Atlantic Coast Express, the Golden Arrow, the Night Ferry, the Bournemouth Belle and of course the Brighton Belle replacing the Southern Belle and becoming the world's first multiple-unit electric Pullman train. Since the 1960s the Southern Region of BR has lost its West of England main line and it is virtually no more than a commuter railway. The Pullmans have vanished, even on boat trains, and Exeter is reached only by a semi-fast diesel service traversing what is now a very secondary route of the Western Region beyond Salisbury. One wonders what Herbert Walker would say if he were still alive!

Whether Walker intended to electrify all the long-distance main lines of the South Western Division, and the relatively lightly-trafficked secondary lines, is doubtful, though it was clear that he wanted to take the third rail over both the Kent Coast main routes. The war of course halted all such plans, and in the interim years between the end of the war and nationalisation, the Southern Railway produced a plan, in which Walker had a hand, for post-war development which provided for electrification of all main routes east of a line from Reading to Portsmouth, with introduction of diesel traction upon secondary lines and branches. This eventually was carried out by the Southern Region with the addition of electrification of the Bournemouth line. Then steam disappeared from the Southern; West of England services were concentrated upon Paddington, and the old LSWR main line to Salisbury and Exeter was relegated to a very secondary position, which would have been inconceivable to Willie Shortt, the outstanding permanent way engineer of the Western District who kept the West of England main line in such perfect condition.

In the tale of the Southern Railway's achievements there are of course some points that can be criticised. In the design of rolling stock for the electrified inner suburban services the Southern seemed old-fashioned compared with the Underground, although traffic on, say, the South London line or the Hounslow loop was hardly distinguishable from that on the District Line. The Southern management was wedded to conventional compartment stock with swing doors, on the theory that only thereby could the maximum number of seats for any given train length be provided, and station stops be limited to a maximum duration of 30 seconds. There were strong counter-arguments to this. Standing in non-corridor compartment stock, when the density of traffic enforces this upon passengers, is quite appallingly uncomfortable, and where loading or unloading at stations is mainly a one-way flow, as on the Southern suburban lines, the use of wide power-operated sliding doors – as the Eastern Region proved conclusively with their Shenfield electrification after the war – leads to station stops just as short as trains with swing doors, sometimes shorter.

Again, if a very long view had been taken, and long-distance main line electrification had been studied from the outset, it is possible that overhead electrification, probably at 1,500 or 3,000 volts d.c., would have proved the better solution. (At that time, of course, the design of electric motors did not make the use of single-phase alternating current at high voltage and 50 Hz industrial frequency a practical proposition.) Admittedly, on the SECR lines restricted clearances would have militated, on cost grounds, against the overhead system.

The mixture of steam and electric traction on the Southern pushed up steam traction costs, since it was left with, broadly, the short and slow movement tasks where economic utilisation could not be achieved. Not until the early 1940s did the Southern produce its first electric locomotives.

A minor criticism of Southern policy is in the realm of aesthetics. SR publicity was always effective but a trifle brash compared with, say, the LNER's use of a distinguished type face, and the dignified LMS posters. And those Southern stations that were effectively modernised, such as Surbiton, Twickenham, Wimbledon, Richmond, Exeter (Central) and Southampton (Central), as well as the new stations on the Wimbledon–Sutton and Chessington branches, while fully adequate for their purpose were not architecturally distinguished. They were perhaps contemporary, vaguely reflecting the idiom of the super-cinema of the 1920s. The widespread use of reinforced concrete in their construction has not withstood the effects of time and weather very well.

For a short-haul line the Southern produced a more than adequate level of train catering through the use of contractors – the Pullman Car Co on the South Eastern and Central (Brighton) Divisions, and Frederick Hotels (who succeeded Spiers and Pond) on the South Western. Walker, as his biographers have pointed out, felt that the business of railwaymen was to provide transport and that if outside experts could be found to look after the ancillary task of selling food and drink – and guarantee a rental payment – so much the better.

If the Southern was happy to hive off its train and station

catering, that certainly was not true of its attitude to its ships and harbours. All three main constituent railways had been proud of their cross-Channel services, and the Southern continued and extended this tradition, in particular by the introduction of train ferry services for sleeping cars and freight wagons. The very high level of traffic on the short sea routes during the summer peaks was profitable and received intensive management attention, and in the days before air travel there was also a steady all year round flow of business travellers to the Continent. 'Roll-on/roll-off' road vehicle ferries to the Isle of Wight were introduced as early as 1928.

Regarding the shipping services as merely a prolongation of a rail service, with the packet ports as ancillary features, was not purely a Southern attitude; each of the other main line companies shared it. But the Southern was unique in also owning and developing a great ocean liner port at Southampton. The association of the LSWR with Southampton was one of long standing. As an ocean terminal the port had its ups and downs although the railway steamers to Normandy, Brittany and the Channel Isles had never deserted it. But it was the Southern Railway's courage and determination in deciding to reclaim a huge area of land and establish the up-to-date Western Docks, with its excellent road and rail access, that really put Southampton firmly in the top league with London, Liverpool, Glasgow and Hull.

Those who participated in management during the long period of Southern emergence look back on the time as a happy if strenuous one. All historians of the railway owe a great debt to Sir John Elliot who joined the Southern in the public relations field in 1925 for a fascinating article he wrote about the early days on the Southern in the *Journal of Transport History* in November 1960. Elliot reminds us that at the outset, some relics of inter-company hostility remained, though nothing comparable to the North Western and Midland enmity on the LMS. The first Continental Traffic Manager, F.A. Brant, who was an ex-SECR man, always tried to avoid travelling on the South Western if possible, while Frank Bushrod, a tough ex-LSWR man who eventually became the Southern Railway Operating Superintendent, always referred to the South Eastern as 'that rag-bag railway'.

But these were quirks that soon faded away, and the team spirit engendered by Walker was quite remarkable. Hardly a breath of criticism seems to have been raised by anyone who ever worked under him. He was a quiet man, dignified without pomposity, reserved yet friendly, a professional to his finger-tips, living for the railway that, in its present form, was largely his creation. Had he accepted the offer from Sir Guy Granet to become General Manager of the LMS at the grouping, which to an ex-LNWR man must have been tempting, he would have resolved the power struggles on that line, and put it on a firmly based policy of modernisation, more quickly than was actually the case, at any rate until Stamp arrived. Even thereafter he would, with his grasp of finance as well as his mastery of traffic questions, by no means have been outshone by Stamp despite the latter's formidable intellectual powers.

Walker was succeeded by the breezy, forthright Gilbert Szlumper who had been his Assistant General Manager ever since 1925. Szlumper carried on the Walker policies but soon the second world war put a stop to planning and the Southern was stretched to the limit to cope with evacuation and Government priority traffics. Szlumper went to the War Office and Eustace Missenden, who had been an effective Docks & Marine Manager, and Traffic Manager, was appointed to replace him.

At the end of the war planning was resumed but nationalisation intervened before most of the plans could be translated into action. For a time the results of what had been achieved in the 1920s and 1930s still provided an adequate standard of service, but any lead over the other main lines was progressively lost as equipment fell due for renewal. The very scale of the new works under Walker made the costs of replacement

Above: *The 'mechanical horse' for railway cartage operations demonstrating its ability to turn and back in a confined space* (Crown copyright, National Railway Museum)

Below: *Road/rail co-ordination: a GWR household removals container* (British Rail)

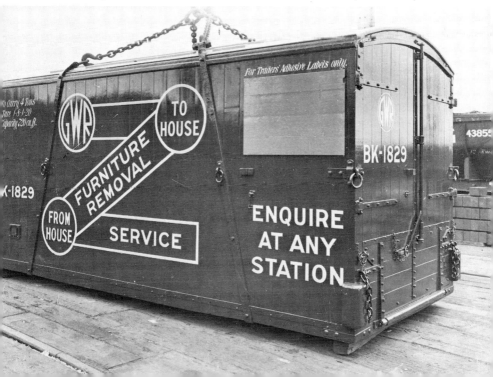

Above: *Classic Great Western: the Riviera about to leave Paddington behind a Star class 4-6-0 a year or so before the grouping, and seen from the spotter's favourite stance on platform 1. Note the all-maroon train livery and the milk churns not yet banished to platform A round the corner* (British Rail)

Below: *The Riviera, but in the 1930s: the engine is now a King and beside it stands one of those surprisingly modern-looking AEC railcars* (British Rail)

formidable and, paradoxically enough, if the Southern Region is today bedevilled with rolling stock and services that do not match up to the best in other Regions of British Rail, this is due largely to its long 'honeymoon' between 1924 and 1937 – the Walker era.

CHAPTER 6

Great Men and Great Engines

The history of mechanical engineering on railways in Britain up to the grouping in 1923 is fascinating, largely because it is so varied, so often coloured by the personalities of the engineers themselves – some autocrats and prima donnas, some comparatively modest men, but all characterised by a devotion to the steam locomotive as something more than an inanimate piece of machinery. Some certainly indulged their own interests and hobby-horses at the expense of the railways' shareholders; others produced economical work-horses that, year after year, helped to earn the dividends. None would agree with old Charles Beyer, founder of the great private engine building firm of Beyer Peacock, when he grunted 'Ach, anything will for a locomotive do'.

After the grouping each of the main line railways can be considered fortunate in its Chief Mechanical Engineer, though the LMS had to wait until 1932 to find the man it really needed. By Stanier, Collett, Gresley and Maunsell the demands of the Operating Departments for traction were well met. The next generation divides into those successors who, by and large, carried on the tradition of their predecessors – Hawksworth on the GWR, Fairburn and Ivatt on the LMS – and those who struck out a new line, Bulleid on the Southern and, to a rather lesser extent, Thompson on the LNER. Another possible division is between those concerned primarily with advanced design – Bulleid especially – and those as much concerned with ease of maintenance, especially Thompson.

So much has been written on locomotive design and locomotive performance in those years that there is little point in adding to the writings. Experts like Cecil J. Allen and O.S. Nock have recorded a profusion of data, and, more recently, the professional locomotive engineers' experience and view-point have come across in books written by distinguished officers after their retirement, such as those by E.S. Cox and Roland Bond – not to mention the racy autobiographies of some engine-drivers such as Norman McKillop.

What perhaps remains, is to try to draw some general con-clusions about the great engineers of the railways. A point sometimes overlooked is that when a locomotive is described as having been 'designed' by Mr X as CME, the actual extent to which Mr X was personally involved in the design – though not, of course, his official responsibility for its success or the reverse – could vary enormously. A Chief Mechanical Engineer was the manager of a very big department in which the design office was only one component and, in terms of staff numbers, not a very large one. By far the greatest work load on the CME's department was not new construction at all, but maintenance. Light, intermediate and heavy repairs to huge fleets of steam locomotives constituted a major indust-rial activity.

Again, carriage and wagon construction and maintenance, with much the heaviest load falling on maintenance, was a major responsibility of the CME, together with a vast amount of ancillary machinery including cranes and pumps and so forth, all over the system. For example, on the LNER the Docks Machinery Engineer and the Road Motor Engineer, controlling a huge fleet of collection and delivery vehicles, came under the CME.

So any view of a typical CME as a man devoting most of his time to dreaming up designs for bigger and better locomotives would be unrealistic. One has to envisage a busy departmen-tal manager, supervising the overall performance of very large workshops, settling staff problems, and frequently dealing constantly with policy questions with such colleagues as the

91

General Manager, the Chief Accountant, the Operating Superintendent and – very important – the Motive Power Superintendent. In addition the Board and the Locomotive Committee would need his presence, perhaps every month, to enlarge upon reports and to justify proposals for expenditure.

Conferences and discussions, examination of drawings and instructions to draughtsmen certainly took place whenever a new type of locomotive was required, but the imprint of the single individual mind of a CME had to be transmitted through a departmental organisation in which modifications and even quite substantial changes might originate. The most successful compounding system used in Britain was devised by W.M. Smith, the influential Chief Draughtsman of the North Eastern Railway, and adopted by Wilson Worsdell on the NER, and by Johnson, Deeley and Fowler on the Midland Railway. In this special case, the real originator's name, and not that of the CME, is applied to the system, but that is exceptional.

A CME, in short, had to be a businessman and not merely a technician, and the little publicised but vital work in the drawing office would often be guided mainly by the Chief Draughtsman, working of course on lines agreed with the CME if not always originating from him.

Lord Chandos, who was trained as an engineer but rose to the Chairmanship of a huge combine, once remarked that a top manager in an engineering business was unlikely to be able to devote more than about 10 per cent of his time to purely engineering matters; 90 per cent was likely to be taken up by administration. A CME, even if a dedicated locomotive engineer, always had to struggle against this tendency for paper work to tie him to his desk.

This creeping trend to bureaucracy was much accentuated by the size of the four group companies compared with their predecessors. It is therefore perhaps surprising that the great CME's of the inter-war years and their show pieces – the new designs of express passenger locomotives – caught the public imagination as much as was the case. It was no doubt partly due to the enterprise of the railways' publicity departments – or public relations departments as they began to be called – in exploiting the publicity value of new locomotives and in claiming, on the rather dubious basis of the formula for calculating nominal tractive effort, to have produced 'the most powerful passenger locomotive in Great Britain'. This not very meaningful title was applied to the GWR Castle class in 1925 during the exchange trials with the LNER in which Gresley's earlier Pacific design did not show to very great advantage; a year later, the Southern's Lord Nelson 4–6–0 claimed the title. Then the LMS pushed up the nominal tractive effort of the Royal Scot class which in some ways resembled the Nelsons, by adopting a high boiler pressure, largely to enable the claim of 'most powerful' to be made. By 1927 the GWR had again jumped ahead by producing an enlarged Castle class, which the publicity people immediately proclaimed as the 'King of railway locomotives', on the basis of its tractive effort statistics.

In fact, looking back, one may feel that in many cases the palm should be awarded to some slightly less glamorous locomotive types that, day in and day out, served the needs of the traffic departments most economically and efficiently as, for example, the Baby Scots or Patriots and Stanier's Black Fives on the LMS; Gresley's maids-of-all-work, the V2 2–6–2 class; the incomparable Great Western Castles that put in nearly 40 years of sterling service; and the splendid Southern Schools class of 4–4–0s, in some ways surpassing both the King Arthurs and the Lord Nelsons.

Of course, the limelight shone on Stanier's splendid Princess Royal and Coronation Pacifics in the later 1930s, as it did on Gresley's streamlined A4 Pacifics. But one must look a little critically at some of the high spots. Stanier could not get the Coronation Scot to Glasgow in less than 6½ hours, half an hour longer than the Coronation took to reach Edinburgh from King's Cross. On the other hand, *Mallard*'s world record of 126mph with steam was achieved downhill, over no more than a quarter of a mile, and – sad to relate – ran a bearing so hot that the engine had to come off at Peterborough instead of continuing to London.

So there was a certain artificiality about the claims made by competing publicity departments. Can one in fact say that steam locomotive design reached its peak of development between the wars? One thing that emerges is the orthodoxy of the principal designs. Compounding, apart from an Indian summer for the Midland 4–4–0 designs of W.M. Smith as perpetuated by Fowler, was out. Feed-water heating and ultra-high boiler pressures were out; the experiment with the latter on the LMS with *Fury* whose water-tube boiler exploded with disastrous results, was an almost isolated example. Turbine propulsion was really confined to the single LMS prototype 'Turbomotive' No 6202, which performed well, though demanding specialised maintenance which led to its eventual reconstruction by British Railways as a Princess Royal Pacific. Gresley produced a one-off design in No 10000, again with a water-tube boiler, a four-cylinder 4–6–4 of striking appearance and – surprising for a former Great Northern man – compounding, which that railway had tried only once, on an Ivatt Atlantic. This impressive locomotive had maintenance troubles and eventually was rebuilt in a similar form to an A4 Pacific though retaining its four trailing wheels.

By and large, the trend of locomotive design among the four great railways was for simple expansion and relatively conventional designs but, for the more powerful machines, with three-cylinder propulsion, except on the GWR where four cylinders were preferred. Boiler pressures had settled down between 200 and 250 lb/sq in and superheating was standard.

By the mid to late 1930s each of the companies seemed well satisfied with the motive power at its command. On the LNER, shortage of funds had prevented standardisation by large building programmes of fewer classes and on the Southern the march of electrification was leading to the cascading of steam locomotives from newly electrified routes – for instance, the departure in 1937 of Schools class engines from the Waterloo–Portsmouth line where they had been putting up some notable performances. On the GWR, the fleet of express passenger locomotives of classic Swindon design was being supplemented by mixed traffic engines of the same general characteristics but with smaller driving wheels and two cylinders – the Halls and Granges, together with a curious throwback to a relatively antique design, the Dukedogs, a rebuilt 4–4–0 type with outside coupling rods reminding one of that Edwardian era when *City of Truro* had made history.

Then came the second world war and utility replaced glamour as the main criterion. Trains of 600 tons or more were common on Anglo-Scottish routes and an overall speed limit of 60 mph was enforced. Cleaning, apart from the motion, was abandoned. Maintenance standards fell sharply.

In the midst of this era came an extraordinary phenomenon – Oliver Bulleid's prototype Merchant Navy Pacific express passenger locomotive, rather disingenuously described as a mixed traffic engine to get round the ruling of the Ministry of War Transport against building passenger locomotives for the period of the emergency. These remarkable machines were magnificent steam-producers, but their highly original chain-driven valve gear was difficult to maintain and drank oil in large quantities, as well as producing difficulties in starting. But Bulleid's Merchant Navies, and their smaller, lighter sisters, the West Country Pacifics, were the last really original designs to be produced in quantity for the main line railways before nationalisation.

The LMS built a few engines after the war very much in the Stanier tradition; the Great Western did not depart far from the path indicated by Churchward and Collett. On the LNER the Thompson régime was interesting, because Edward

Thompson underlined the potential weakness of Gresley's famous locomotive classes – the imprecision of valve events for the middle cylinder after wear had taken place, and the tendency for middle big-ends to run hot. He used these as arguments for rebuilding Gresley engines with separate sets of valve gear, and for confining his own new mixed traffic designs to two cylinders.

In fairness to Gresley, it was a combination of over-loading and poor wartime maintenance that made these troubles so conspicuous. Thompson's policy of building medium-powered locomotives of classic 4–6–0 design, easy to maintain, was probably correct in the context of wartime and post-war requirements.

One last fling of originality, before nationalisation – and the BR standard designs – descended upon the railways, was the bold if misguided attempt by Bulleid to design a steam locomotive that would render dieselisation – perhaps in some cases even electrification – unnecessary. This was the Leader class, conceived as a sort of general-purpose steam motive power unit rivalling Alfred Raworth's CC1 and CC2 prototype electric locomotives, with 100 per cent adhesion and driving cabs at each end like an electric locomotive, though the fireman had to work in a central compartment which heated up to an intolerable extent. This conception of a double-bogie steam locomotive, with sleeve-valve cylinders, chain-coupled driving wheels and an offset boiler with thermic syphons instead of a firebox, was a late fling by a truly original mind tackling the problems of steam traction without regard to the past. Its failure in trials forms a tragi-comic finale to a period of 25 years during which steam traction remained basically conventional but probably touched the highest level of achievement feasible before economic and social conditions rendered the search for other forms of motive power inevitable.

At this point one must ask if the great men of the steam age were purblind in virtually ignoring the inevitable – the supersession of steam by oil and electricity. On the Southern this problem hardly arose; Bulleid and Raworth were well aware of each other's place in the scheme of things as laid down by Herbert Walker. The LMS did not take electrification very seriously, but several experiments with oil engines were made. A three-car train set with Leyland diesel engines and hydraulic transmission introduced in 1938 worked for some time between Oxford and Cambridge via Bletchley. This was less successful than the diesel-electric 0–6–0 shunters, which performed admirably. The LMS's energetic Road Motor Engineer, John Shearman, pioneered a 'Ro-Railer', a sort of bus that could run on either pneumatic tyres or a flanged wheel, that travelled by rail between Blisworth and Stratford-on-Avon, continuing by road to the LMS Welcombe Hotel at the latter place.

The LNER had a fleet of steam railcars among which was included a single oil-engined unit, the *Tyneside Venturer*, and the GWR had its fleet of AEC diesel railcars. But, by and large, diesel traction was a cloud no bigger than a man's hand upon a horizon of unlimited steam traction, until the end of the war. Then each company began seriously to consider the future. The Southern and the LMS each ordered two proto-type diesel-electric locomotives, while the LNER had its bold scheme for 25, to replace steam on the East Coast Main Line. The GWR, always determined to be different, ordered two gas-turbine prototypes. All this was to be brushed aside after nationalisation, when, under a Railway Executive department mainly drawn from the LMS, steam embarked upon its illusory Indian summer in a world that had changed fundamentally since the great days of Churchward and Collett, Stanier, Maunsell, and Gresley.

CHAPTER 7

What did the Passenger get?

The lifetime of the four great railways comprised a decade and a half of peacetime progress followed by a decade of war and the aftermath of war. In this second phase the passenger often had to accept such rail transport as was available, even if slow, unpunctual and overcrowded, because the alternatives were so restricted. In the earlier and historically more interesting phase, between the wars, what the passenger was given needs to be related to the strength of competition from other means of transport.

Broadly, the railways remained, for all but short journeys, the backbone system of passenger transport. The number of cars registered in 1925 was 580,000, and by 1939 it had increased to 2 million, which at the time seemed rapid growth, but compared with the 1978 total of 15 million, it hardly suggests very serious competition with the railways. Nor were the companies very concerned to woo motorists back to rail; the growth of long-distance motor coach travel, was taken rather more seriously, but in the absence of motorways the speed of coach travel fell far below that of express trains. Journeys by the four main line railways were 1,319 million in 1923, and 1,210 million in 1937, a fall of little more than 8 per cent.

Passenger fares were normally based on distance, though not quite so rigidly as on the Continent where, if one knew the distance, it was often simple to calculate the fare. There were various apparent anomalies, including the special fares over 'competitive routes' by which the fare over a longer distance was the same as that by the shortest route. Standardised fares such as London to Glasgow from Euston, St Pancras or King's Cross, or London to Manchester from Euston, St Pancras or Marylebone reflected not merely the agreements to end competition in fares but the pooling schemes established in 1928.

The standard third-class single fare was fixed at 1½d (about 0.6p) in 1923 and the first-class fare at 2½d (about 1p) per mile. There they remained for a long time, the railways considering that increases would not improve total receipts but reduce them through a disproportionate fall in the number of passengers. Return fares were normally twice the single fare, but a number of special concession fares existed – for example, tourist tickets, week-end tickets at the single fare and a third, and excursion tickets available only on special excursion trains. Half-day excursions on Sundays were very popular, with fares ranging from about 10s (50p) to 4s (20p).

With falling traffics, however, the railways took a bold step. The validity of week-end tickets was extended to a month, a period within which the great majority of return journeys were made. At first this was during the summer only and the tickets were called 'Summer Return Tickets', but as the experiment was considered a success it was made permanent and the tickets were re-christened 'Monthly Returns'; much stress was laid, in publicity material, on the fact that this represented a fare of approximately one (old) penny a mile, at which rail travel was cheap.

In return for their fares, passengers for some time after 1923 were not able to travel as fast as they had done in 1914. It sometimes seemed as though the grouped companies, preoccupied with internal problems of reorganisation, had little interest in regaining the standard set by their predecessors; this was markedly the case where the LMS and the LNER were concerned, while the GWR had never laid much emphasis on speed except as regards a handful of its crack trains. By comparison, the Southern did slightly better.

Year after year in *The Railway Magazine*, writing under the pen-name of 'Voyageur', Cecil J. Allen analysed the summer service of express trains from London to principal cities and demonstrated how the best performances of 1914 were still not being equalled. Such a comparison of course was not complete; it did not illustrate service frequency or the other features, such as availability of restaurant cars.

But it was a pretty depressing tale. For instance, in the summer of 1924, Allen showed that out of 64 express train services between London and major provincial centres, 13 were as fast as but no faster than 10 years previously, 16 were faster, but no less than 35 were slower than before the war. There were also fewer non-stop runs of 100 miles or over (130 against 138 pre-war), and Allen concluded that 'the general average of these figures worked out at 23·4 per cent, or practically 14 minutes added to every hour of travelling, as compared with pre-war figures'.

Five years later, in 1929, a similar survey (conducted from now on by Allen under the pen-name of 'Mercury') produced a result showing that services were overall still 1 per cent slower than in 1914. For the four groups, the results were:

GWR	3·18 per cent faster
SR	0·65 per cent faster
LNER	1·12 per cent slower
LMS	2·86 per cent slower

It was pointed out by 'Mercury' that the GWR improvement had been effected 'chiefly by the acceleration of certain selected crack trains, rather than by that of the express services as a whole', while on the Southern 'there has not only been a quickening of minimum times, but also a levelling-up of express timings in general . . . the Southern has made greater all-round improvements of its train services since the war than any other British group'.

The worst showing, year after year, had been on the Midland Division of the LMS, a surprising result in view of

100

the extent of Midland influence in the top echelons of that railway including the adoption of the Midland's operating organisation, much to the disgust of the ex-LNWR element. The Midland's best time to Manchester was still 4 hours compared with 3 hours 40 minutes in 1914 and to Leeds, 3 hours 52 minutes compared with 3 hours 40 minutes. Moreover the Midland's pre-1914 non-stop runs from St Pancras to Chinley (169½ miles), St Pancras to Shipley (206 miles) and St Pancras to Nottingham (123½ miles) were not revived.

One must wonder why the railways, with the honourable exception of the Southern, appeared so uninterested in exploiting their speed potential as a means of retaining or increasing their long-distance passenger traffic. Even on the progressive Southern, on its heavily-used Brighton main line, the standard published time from London to Brighton was still the 60 minutes that had been the best performance with steam, though with electrification it was performed every hour from early morning until midnight; in addition some trains had a working timetable schedule of 55 minutes, though this was not publicly advertised. When electrification was carried to Portsmouth via Haslemere in 1937 the standard timing for the hourly fast trains was 90 minutes – a time which the Schools class steam locomotives had already kept, and from time to time bettered, on this route, as Cecil J. Allen recorded in *The Railway Magazine* in February 1936 – though the electrics had a couple of intermediate stops.

In frequency of service, the picture is a more encouraging one. Wherever the Southern electrified, a more frequent and regular service followed. Even where steam trains were slower than in 1914, they tended to be more frequent. The Midland Division of the LMS, although taking 4 hours from St Pancras to Manchester against 3 hours 40 minutes pre-war, instituted a clock-face service at 25 minutes past the hour, with departures every two hours (with very few gaps) from 4.25am until the evening.

The clock-face principle crept in only gradually. The GWR's use of it has already been mentioned. For many years the LSWR had (with steam traction) a tradition, continued by the Southern, that the best West of England trains left Waterloo at the hour, the Bournemouth trains at 30 minutes past and the Portsmouth trains at 50 minutes past. It was a pity that this principle was not more universally applied.

So far as passenger comfort is concerned, the riding qualities of passenger stock are a product not merely of good bogie design but also, very emphatically, of the quality of the permanent way. Before the grouping, many people considered that the Midland carried off the palm for smooth-riding vehicles with, in particular, its splendid Bain 12-wheeled dining carriages, though the best LNWR 12-wheeled stock from Wolverton, such as the famous Corridor (afternoon Anglo-Scottish service) train set, was probably its equal; moreover the North Western permanent way was claimed in the company's advertisements to be the best in the world. The Great Northern's main line stock designed by Gresley with double bolster bogies, if well maintained, rode well, and the long-standing tradition of deep ballasting, even covering the tops of the sleepers, gave GN track a very high reputation. So too, of course, was that of the Great Western; bowling along Brunel's magnificently aligned main line was almost always a smooth and enjoyable experience even if the GWR rolling stock was capriciously variable in its characteristics.

After the grouping there was a general levelling-up of standards where they had previously been unsatisfactory, particularly on the Southern Railway, rather than any major advance in super-comfort. Indeed, the mass-produced all-steel LMS main line carriages of the mid-1920s were scarcely as smooth-riding as the best MR and LNWR stock. The search for economy through reducing tare weight was detrimental to ideal riding quality, though there was no serious cause for complaint – at any rate, at speeds up to 70 miles an hour or thereabouts. Riding could be rough on vehicles due for a visit to main shops, if speeds were much higher.

Gresley's articulated main line sets rode well on the whole, though not as smoothly as his single vehicles; all the main line stock built with the buckeye coupler whose use he pioneered, with much justification, was liable to jerk at starting as the slight slack in the couplers was taken up. But only the LNER and the Southern adopted the buckeye coupler as standard, despite its marked advantages in a mishap.

There were some curious survivals of veteran stock, one of the most striking being the LMS North London close-coupled sets of four-wheelers, built with wooden seats in third class compartments, some of which still ran in their NLR teak livery on the Broad Street–Poplar service as late as 1938. The North London trains and the LNER London suburban services were almost the last to retain second class accommodation. In 1937 it completely disappeared except on Continental boat trains, where it was argued that so long as the Continental railways maintained three classes, the connecting services must do also – despite the fact that almost all the steamers were two-class only!

Minor aspects of passenger comfort were lighting and heating, where progress in the 1920s was steady rather than spectacular. Shoulder lights for reading comfort began to appear in main line stock, though the change from gas to electric lighting was not complete even by the date of nationalisation, when the companies handed over 3,686 gas-lit vehicles to British Railways. Standards improved with through lighting control switched on and off by the guard, which normally ensured that all lights were on before tunnels were entered. Steam heating was practically universal with steam traction, the hot-water footwarmers of earlier days having disappeared along with the oil lamps that used to be dropped into position with a thunderous noise as trains waited at stations.

Carriage design remained pretty conservative. Non-corridor compartment stock was still being built for local and short-distance journeys; it could be very austere, as in Gresley's articulated suburban sets – 'quads' and 'quins' – and some other close-coupled suburban rakes.

Main line corridor carriages continued to be built of traditional side-corridor compartment design in the 1920s until in 1925 the LMS created a mild sensation by introducing for the St Pancras to Bradford service a new corridor train composed entirely of open coaches vestibuled to a kitchen car, so that meals could be served at every seat. This heralded a gradual move towards the greater use of open saloon type stock with less emphasis placed on the so-called 'privacy' of the compartment design dating back to the earliest days of railways. The Southern, although adhering to compartment stock for suburban services, from the outset provided both open and compartment stock for its main line electrification schemes, as well as some of its steam-hauled services. In steam stock, Gresley built for the LNER a series of excursion sets of open vehicles, and he included open saloons in the prestige vehicles he built for the high speed trains and other special services such as the Hook Continental, and the East Anglian. Even the conservative Great Western built in 1935 two ten-coach excursion train sets with open stock, vestibuled to kitchen cars from which meals were served at every seat, though open stock other than for dining purposes was not provided normally by the GWR between the wars.

One measure in which the four companies failed to agree was the improvement of passenger comfort in third-class compartments of main line corridor stock, by providing armrests to divide compartments into three-a-side seating, instead of the previously standard four-a-side. The armrests could, however, be raised flush with the seat backs, thus allowing four-a-side seating at times of peak traffic.

The LMS and LNER accepted this principle, considering that it would promote travel through the extra space and comfort provided for third class passengers who comprised the great majority of rail travellers. The GWR and the

Above: *Untypical of the GWR, the experimental articulated twin-set for main line working* (British Rail)

Below: *Gresley's A4 Pacifics are in some ways the LNER trademark; yet they only show the classic elegance of their lines when viewed from the side and are stationary* (Crown copyright, National Railway Museum)

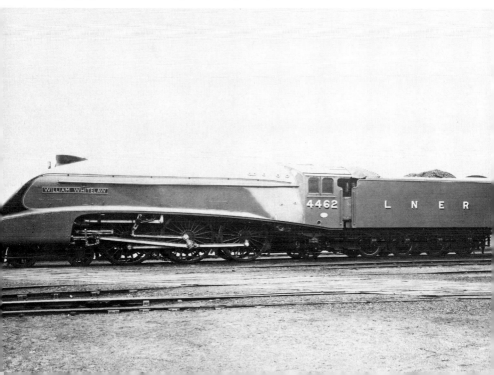

Above: *An unusual combination: Gresley's high-pressure water-tube boiler 4-6-4 No 10000 at the head of the Flying Scotsman* (Crown copyright, National Railway Museum)

Below: *A small-boilered Ivatt Atlantic on an up Cambridge express before the inauguration of the 'Beer Trains'* (L&GRP/David & Charles)

Southern objected; they maintained that only three seats a side would be a serious handicap at the holiday peak seasons, and that there would be disputes among passengers as to whether the armrests should be raised to provide additional seats by 'crowding up'. In consequence, they adhered to four a side, a policy lasting for some years after nationalisation when BR standard coaches were built with three-a-side or four-a-side seating depending on regional allocation.

Facilities for meals on trains increased steadily up to the outbreak of war in 1939. In 1924 there were 637 daily restaurant or Pullman car services; by 1929 this had increased to 740. The traditional set menus continued to be served at breakfast, lunch, tea and dinner, only the Pullman services on the Southern and LNER, and the buffet cars on the LNER, breaking away to give à la carte service.

An example of a typical Midland 'Dining Carriage' luncheon menu of the 1920s (price 3s 6d [17½p], with coffee 4d [1½p] extra) would be:

Green pea soup
Boiled turbot and boiled potatoes
Roast mutton, redcurrant jelly, roast potatoes,
cauliflower, carrots
Cabinet pudding
Cheese, biscuits and celery

To increase business, however, the GWR instituted an alternative shorter luncheon menu at 2s6d (12½p) consisting of a main course and sweet, which reflected the steady trend to less substantial eating habits.

The Great Eastern Railway had a tradition of good catering which survived under the LNER. The cellars of the Great Eastern Hotel were famous for their wines, and the GER had supported its restaurant car services, as well as its hotels, by running its own bakery and also a farm.

The services provided by the independent Pullman Car

Company were curiously localised. They were widespread on the Southern and LNER, non-existent on the LMS (in later years), and also on the GWR except for the short-lived experiments with the Torquay Pullman and Pullman cars in the Plymouth Ocean Liner specials. (Oddly enough, the GWR afterwards built for these trains some saloon coaches that were almost replicas of Pullman designs.)

Pullman cars had of course been introduced in Britain on the Midland Railway's Anglo-Scottish services as sleeping cars. They had ceased to operate on this route long before the grouping, but the LMS in 1923 inherited from the Caledonian an agreement with the Pullman Company to provide services in Scotland, mostly in non-supplement restaurant cars. After the grouping the LMS had some of these vehicles transferred for a time to other routes (ex-Highland and Glasgow & South Western) pending expiry of the agreement, when it purchased the Pullman cars – which the Pullman Company was unable to re-deploy elsewhere – at rock-bottom prices, and operated them for some time as ordinary restaurant cars.

The LNER inherited substantial agreements with Pullman from the Great Eastern Railway, and it developed and re-arranged the Pullman workings on routes that seemed to have a higher revenue potential – London to the West Riding, to Scotland via Leeds and Harrogate, and for a short time, to Sheffield via Nottingham from King's Cross. Many Great Eastern section cars, in fact, were thus transferred by the LNER to the Great Northern section very soon after the grouping, leaving only the cars for the Harwich (Parkeston Quay) boat trains and the Eastern Belle excursions.

The Southern had inherited from two of its constituent companies extensive agreements with Pullman which it also developed and re-arranged. It made widespread use of a single Pullman car in a fixed rake of main-line vehicles to provide a catering service, as well as operating a few all-Pullman trains such as the Brighton Belle and the Bournemouth Belle. Refreshment service was sometimes provided by

108

a pantry car built by the Southern, but staffed by Pullman crews. This was partly due to the difficulty the Pullman Car Company experienced in justifying the construction of Pullman vehicles for services where the catering demand was relatively light. In fact, Pullman generally reckoned that the all-Pullman trains were profitable, but single cars in trains of ordinary stock were barely if at all profitable especially after the introduction of corridor trains on relatively short runs, enabling passengers in an ordinary compartment to buy refreshments from the Pullman attendants without paying a supplement. Most notable of Southern Pullman trains was the Golden Arrow, instituted in 1929, a first-class-only Pullman service between London and Paris in 6 hours 35 minutes with a special steamer, the *Canterbury*, that made the crossing from Dover to Calais in 75 minutes. However, Pullman cars in boat trains had been a feature since 1910 and, before the Golden Arrow, substantial rakes of Pullmans were working in connection with the Continental sailings.

Pullman standards were maintained by a tradition under which the management closely supervised the services to ensure that quality was maintained. The Pullman conductors were men of authority and stature, all personally known to the inspectors and General Manager. It is interesting that between the wars, with the financial problems in retaining family personal servants, the Pullman Company were successful in recruiting several 'gentlemen's gentlemen' for their travelling staff.

Pullman catering, even though frequently provided from tiny kitchens which imposed a pretty limited choice of dishes upon the menu, always had a certain panache, an impression of willingness to satisfy any whim of the passenger whenever he might require food or drink, in contrast to the more regimented summons to the dining car table d'hôte which the railway restaurant car service practised. (The Pullman Company at one time advertised that special meals could be served by notice in advance.)

Sleeping car services for a time lagged behind the standard of 1914; in 1924, for example, there were only 60 compared with 68 just before the war. However, the building of new cars soon improved the position and by 1929 there were 72 nightly services with first class cars (some on the LNER including showers) and 48 with third class cars.

A major change had come in September 1928, when agreement was reached (after some long debates in the Railway Clearing House) by the LMS, LNER and GWR to introduce third-class sleepers. These were officially described as providing lying-down accommodation only. A number of corridor compartment vehicles were converted or newly built, so that the seats formed two berths, and hinged partitions were let down to provide two further berths on the upper level. Rugs and pillows were provided but no sheets; passengers were not expected to undress or change into nightwear. With four to a compartment, bookings were arranged as far as possible to provide for single-sex occupancy, or for two married couples to share a compartment; it was a policy to which it was not always easy to adhere at times of peak holiday travel.

The companies considered that, on balance, the facility was commercially justified at the charge of 6s (30p) for each berth between stations in England and Wales, or inside Scotland, and 7s (35p) for Anglo-Scottish journeys. (This was probably correct, unless occupancy of say six seats at normal fares could be guaranteed in each compartment.)

The Southern did not participate in this innovation. The LSWR had sold off its sleeping cars built for the Plymouth ocean liner specials after these trains were discontinued in 1910, and it was not until 1936 that sleepers (first class only) re-appeared on Southern metals for the Wagon-Lits Night Ferry to Paris.

From the date of grouping until 1937, progress in the level of passenger services was steady rather than spectacular. In the latter year, however, major improvements in train running were made, above all on the Midland Division of the

110

LMS, largely because of the new locomotive power available as a result of the Stanier régime and the Lemon reforms of the LMS main line timetable.

At last, in his annual review, Cecil J. Allen was able to show that every major division of the four group railways was showing reductions in average journey time compared with 1914. The highest improvement was on the GN section of the LNER, at 15·6 per cent, the East Coast service as a whole being 11·4 per cent faster; the LMS Western Division showed a 10·7 per cent improvement and the Midland Division (at long last) was 3·5 per cent faster. Over the whole 72 services between London and provincial centres, 'Mercury' recorded a saving in journey time of 4¼ minutes in every hour.

The highlights of these services were of course the handful of very high speed trains – the Coronation, West Riding Limited and Silver Jubilee of the LNER, the Coronation Scot of the LMS, and the Cheltenham Flier and Bristolian of the GWR. But more important for most passengers was the smartening of the run-of-the-mill services; it can confidently be said that in 1939 the British rail passenger enjoyed a level of service that represented the best that could be achieved with steam traction, as regards speed, frequency and comfort. Any real further advance would have to depend upon the adoption of new technology – something that did not happen until the 1960s.

CHAPTER 8

Signalling, Safety and Accidents

By the time that the four great railways came into being, the nineteenth-century arguments between the Railway Inspectorate of the Board of Trade, continually pressing for standardisation of safety measures that nowadays seem essential and even elementary, and railway managements too often inclined to drag their feet, were a thing of the distant past. The stragglers had finally been pushed into line by legislation – the Regulation of Railways Act of 1889 – which set deadlines for the adoption of some essential safety measures.

Thus in the twentieth century all major railways followed the four main principles for which the Inspecting Officers had first pleaded and then fought. These were: full interlocking of points and signals; absolute block signalling on all lines used by passenger trains; automatic continuous brakes under the control of the driver; and provision for emergency communication between passengers and the train crew. They were in fact taken for granted, and the obstinate objections to their compulsory introduction that had been raised by a few Victorian railway managers now seemed laughable.

Yet there was not complete standardisation. Block signalling procedures varied from railway to railway and were certainly not fully standard even within each grouped company, since diverging constituent company practices inherited in 1923 were often continued. Nor could it be said that expenditure on safety measures had been directly related to the prosperity of the company. The wealthy London & North Western had clung for much too long to the obsolete Clark and Webb chain brake when other railways had adopted the compressed air or vacuum brake while the impoverished

London, Chatham & Dover had boldly standardised Sykes' lock and block, a substantial improvement on the simple block telegraph, but one that was rather more expensive to install and maintain.

There was, however, no ground for complacency. The appalling Quintinshill disaster in 1915, in which about 217 died (the exact number is unknown), had demonstrated that contemporary signalling procedures and safety precautions were still too dependent upon the human factor. A short lapse of memory, or a failure to carry out some simple measure enjoined by the rule book such as placing a collar over a lever as a reminder of track occupation, could have terrible consequences. In fact, it was a tribute to the conscientiousness and long-standing tradition of discipline among railwaymen, that far more accidents did not take place.

Interlocking of points and signals had ensured that drivers were given accurate information about the setting of the road for their trains. The absolute block system, *if* the procedure was correctly followed, also ensured that drivers were given accurate information about the occupation of the track by other trains. But the possibilities of human error remained; a lapse on the part of a signalman could result in a clear signal being given when a track was in fact occupied, though this was much less likely, and required a much more serious lapse on the signalman's part where lock and block was in force. And, very important, a driver could fail to read the signals correctly and obey them. Lastly, there was the possibility of mechanical failure either on the train, such as the breaking of an axle, or on the track, such as a broken rail or faulty alignment.

With the honourable exception of the Great Western Railway, it cannot be said that there was very striking progress in what may be called the technology of safety between 1923 and 1948. The Great Western extended its so-called Automatic Train Control, better described as Audible Cab Signalling, to all its main lines with beneficial results.

The GWR safety record was particularly good, and after accidents on other lines the Inspecting Officers' reports from time to time observed that accidents could have been prevented, or at least their effects mitigated, had the GWR system been in use.

Rather similar devices to ensure that drivers obeyed a danger signal were not unknown among the other railways. The LNER had inherited from J.G. Robinson, Chief Mechanical Engineer of the Great Central Railway, a device known as 'Reliostop', which was initially installed between Marylebone and Harrow, and later extended. Its characteristics were trip arms on locomotives and treadles operated by the signal wires for both distant and stop signals. It was simple and effective, but after the 1923 grouping its extension was ended when some 40 miles of track had been equipped.

The former North Eastern Railway had laid out an early installation designed by Vincent Raven as early as 1896, which was also simple, being based initially on lineside stop arms like those used on the London Underground, but later on ramps situated between the running rails. Like 'Reliostop', this system, regrettably, was not perpetuated by the LNER after the grouping.

The LMS installed on the busy London, Tilbury & Southend line a variant on the GWR form of ATC known as the Hudd system in which physical contact was replaced by magnetic attraction from a combination of permanent and electro-magnets on the track with the electro-magnet energised to give a clear indication in the cab, de-energised for caution. A fail-safe characteristic was provided, in that the permanent magnet triggered off the system at each location. Much developed and improved, the Hudd type formed the basis of British Rail's Automatic Warning System after nationalisation.

Attempts to improve the reliability of the block system, which depended upon signalmen following a simple procedure under which signals could be cleared only in conformity

114

with indications given audibly by block bells and repeated visually on the block telegraph instruments, were many. The greatest danger was always that a signalman might overlook a train in his section if it were stopped out of course for some reason, perhaps thinking that it must have cleared the section or that he had forgotten or misunderstood a message from the next signal box. Various rules were designed to obviate this risk, such as the obligation to place a collar on a signal lever or the duty of the fireman or guard of a train stopped by signal to go to the signal box and remain there as a continuing human reminder (the former famous Rule 55), but none was entirely proof against the occasional human failure.

There was considerable progress in the replacement of semaphores by colour-light signals which were more conspicuous and gave the same indications by day and by night. The Southern was particularly active in this field and pioneered the use of four-aspect signals which, closely spaced together in congested sections of line, greatly increased line capacity and enabled drivers to run with confidence on close headways. The Southern management in fact maintained that, pound for pound, this yielded more benefit in terms of increased safety than any other single form of expenditure.

A minor change (in which all the railways except the Great Western participated) was the replacement of the standard lower-quadrant semaphore, in which the arm fell to around 45 degrees to indicate clear and rose to the horizontal by the action of a counter-weight to indicate danger, by an upper-quadrant design which was slightly cheaper to construct and maintain. Many also considered that it gave a clearer indication to drivers, and that its return to the horizontal danger position by gravity provided an in-built fail-safe feature through avoiding the need for a counterweight.

Another rationalisation cleared away an anomaly that had existed for many years. In the early days of railways, while red had been the universal danger signal, white had signified clear and green meant caution. Although white had given way to green for the night-time clear indication of semaphore signals from the 1890s the earlier meanings survived in flag signal usage well into the 1920s; a signalman displaying a green flag from his box was instructing a driver that he must proceed at caution. Another anomaly was that the arms of distant signals, which in the horizontal position indicated caution, were painted red like those of stop signals, and were only distinguished by day from the latter by the fishtail cut-out at the end. By night, however, they displayed a red light identical with that of a stop signal; only the driver's route knowledge availed to tell him whether he might pass such a red light or not. Should he mistake his location and believe that a stop signal's red light was that of the distant, the consequences could be serious.

One or two railways, including the London, Brighton & South Coast, had long recognised this problem and distinguished distant signals at night by the use of the Coligny-Welch lamp reflector, which gave a white fish-tail light alongside the red light.

But from the mid-1920s things were tidied up. Yellow was standardised as the colour of distant signal arms (a practice long followed on the open-air sections of the Underground railways) and yellow lights replaced red in distant signals, the first instance having been pioneered by the Great Central Railway before grouping, between Marylebone and Neasden. Flags were also rationalised, green being now used for clear and yellow for caution.

Perhaps the greatest single measure that improved safety during the period, however, was the steady extension of track circuiting, which substituted a positive and unmistakable indication of the occupation of a track by a train for a signalman's possibly fallible observation of his block instruments. When interlocked with signals, it could ensure that they could not give an erroneous indication. Continuous track circuiting is the foundation of sophisticated modern signalling systems and its introduction was fostered by all the four railways.

A noteworthy scheme was the institution in 1933 by the LNER of relay interlocking with continuous track circuiting and route-setting panel switches in the signalboxes, over 25 miles of the main line between York and Northallerton.

Mechanical failures, happily, were becoming far less common that they had been in the 19th century, improved materials and more rigorous inspection procedures playing a major part. But in 1924 a locomotive tyre broke on the LMS at Lytham in Lancashire, and the derailment of the train was followed by a fire causing fourteen passenger deaths.

A combination of faults in the design of a new locomotive class and in the standard of track maintenance was the cause of the Sevenoaks accident on the Southern Railway in 1927. A new class of 2–6–4 tank engine, the River class, had been drafted into express passenger work. Near Sevenoaks on a falling gradient an express from Cannon Street to Deal was derailed at high speed and unfortunately struck the pier of an overbridge which caused the train to jack-knife with much destruction, thirteen passengers being killed. The problem facing the inquiry into the accident was whether the design of the locomotive or poor track was primarily responsible. The General Manager, Sir Herbert Walker, delivered a judgment of Solomon to the departmental officers seeking, naturally enough, to exculpate their own department. He decided that the River class engines should be withdrawn immediately for conversion into tender engines (the surging of water in the side tanks being a probable cause of instability at speed), and that the main line from London to Dover should have the standard of its permanent way uplifted as soon as possible.

In the same year as the Sevenoaks accident there occurred an accident at Hull on the LNER which showed that even modern interlocking was not proof against human error; a collision took place outside Hull Paragon station following a signalman's mistake in which a train left the station on the wrong line and collided head-on with an arriving train, twelve passengers being killed.

In the Charfield disaster in 1928, when an LMS passenger train collided on a misty morning with a GWR goods train being shunted into a siding, there was a presumption that the express train driver had not seen a distant signal at caution though both he and his fireman were positive that the signal had been at clear. The Inspecting Officer emphasised that the GWR system of Automatic Train Control would have prevented this accident, in which fifteen people were killed.

The LNER also experienced a serious accident in 1928 at Darlington when a driver misread a signal and pulled out of a shunting road on to the main line just as a fast excursion train arrived and collided with the departing train at 45 mph, twenty-five passengers being killed.

The LMS was unfortunate in two derailments at speed, one at Leighton Buzzard in 1931 and one at Great Bridgeford in 1932, in each case when drivers failed for some reason to reduce speed properly before being diverted through a crossover from down fast to down slow tracks at Leighton Buzzard, and from up slow to up fast at Great Bridgeford. The casualties fortunately were fewer than might have been the case; in both accidents the reason for the drivers' failure to observe signals correctly remains uncertain.

There was an echo of the 1927 Sevenoaks accident on the Southern in 1933, when a tank engine heading a train at speed was derailed at Raynes Park, on a section of track that was being lifted for maintenance purposes, though in this case the M7 0-4-4 engine class was not suspected of instability such as the River class possessed in their original form.

In 1934 the LMS was again unlucky with two accidents in September: at Port Eglinton near Glasgow a head-on collision took place when the driver, on an engine running tender first, failed to read signals correctly, and at Winwick Junction, a local train standing on the main line was overlooked by a signalman who lowered his signals for a London to Blackpool express which collided at speed with the rear of the local train. At Port Eglinton three enginemen and six passengers were killed; at Winwick ten passengers and the guard of the local train.

The following year the LNER also experienced a rear-end collision at Welwyn Garden City, when a Leeds express travelling at 70 mph crashed into a slowly moving Newcastle express which had been checked by signals but not brought to a standstill at the moment of impact. Thirteen passengers were killed. The cause was not clearly identified though there had clearly been signalmen's errors since the drivers had been obeying the signals quite correctly. The Inspecting Officer of the Ministry of Transport suggested a form of interlocking between track circuits and block instruments to make it impossible for a signalman to accept a second train until the first had occupied and then cleared the home signal track circuit. This procedure, known as 'Welwyn Control', has since been used extensively on main lines retaining manual block working.

Yet another rear-end collision on the LNER took place in 1937, at Castlecary half way between Edinburgh and Glasgow. In a snowstorm an Edinburgh to Glasgow express collided at 60 mph with a stationary train from Dundee to Glasgow, killing 35 passengers. The Inspecting Officer concluded that the conflicting evidence as to the cause of this accident, particularly the indication of a distant signal, showed the need for both Welwyn Control and ATC.

Throughout the period between the wars the safety record of the Great Western Railway had been outstanding. It was sad that so fine a record was broken in 1940 in the unusual accident at Norton Fitzwarren, west of Taunton. A night sleeping car train from Paddington to Penzance ran on a relief line from Taunton station to Norton Fitzwarren Junction, while a newspaper train ran parallel with it on the main line, with signals clear for it to take precedence over the sleeping car train. Unfortunately the driver of the latter misread the signals for the main line as applying to himself and instead of stopping short of the converging junction, ran at speed

119

through trap points and off the road, the train being spread-eagled across the tracks; 27 passengers lost their lives. The ATC apparatus in this case appeared to have been in working order and it seemed that the driver must have received the audible cab signal and cancelled it without acting upon it, a demonstration that even the GWR system of ATC was not 100 per cent proof against human error.

During the war years, 1939–45, information about railway accidents was subject to the censorship regulations. In fact, most mishaps were concerned with enemy activity in one form or another. An exception was the Soham explosion, when a train of 51 wagons loaded with bombs and aircraft components caught fire. The driver and fireman heroically remained with the train, uncoupled the leading wagon which was the one on fire and also loaded with bombs, and drew it past the station hoping to detach it where it could not detonate the remaining wagons. Unhappily the wagon exploded before they could complete this task, the fireman and the station signalman being killed and the driver being seriously injured; the remainder of the train was saved from explosion which would have probably obliterated the town of Soham. Both driver and fireman, the latter posthumously, were awarded the George Cross.

Wartime incidents related to enemy action will be described in a later chapter. Just after the end of the war with Japan, another derailment was caused by excessive speed when an express was diverted over a crossover from up fast to up slow line on the LMS at Bourne End in Hertfordshire. Once more it was a case of an inexplicable failure to read signals correctly on the part of a driver; 36 passengers as well as the driver and fireman were killed.

The LNER was unlucky in 1946 when two trains were derailed at neighbouring locations, Marshmoor and Hatfield on the Great Northern main line, in each case the cause apparently being a combination of faults in track alignment and in riding characteristics of the V2 class of 2–6–2 mixed-traffic locomotives at speed – recalling to some extent the attributed causes of the Southern Railway Sevenoaks accident.

Another derailment, due apparently to permanent way defects – seemingly an aftermath of the reduction in maintenance standards during the war – took place at Polesworth on the LMS Trent Valley line in 1947, when a Liverpool express left the rails at speed on a curve with disastrous consequences, five passengers being killed. Yet another disaster caused by a driver's failure to reduce speed for a diversion from the main line to a subsidiary track, and ignoring signals, took place on the LNER at Goswick between Berwick and Newcastle in October 1947. The 11.15am Edinburgh-King's Cross train was derailed at the turnout and 27 passengers were killed in the last serious accident before the railways were nationalised.

Looking back from 1947 to 1923, it is relevant to wonder whether the group companies did as much as they should have done to improve safety, or whether they were too inclined to rely on long-established procedures and the discipline enjoined by the rule book.

A distinction can properly be drawn between the GWR and the Southern on the one hand, and the LMS and LNER on the other. Too sweeping conclusions should not be drawn from accident statistics, particularly over a short period of years, because of the element of chance. But even so, the safety records of the first two companies do appear significantly better than those of the latter two.

The Great Western had two factors working for it, the family feeling and consequent high sense of responsibility among the staff, and the progressive extension of audible cab signalling to all its main lines. There are of course no figures to show how many accidents on the GWR *might* have taken place in the absence of this device, but there is a long list of accidents on other railways which could have been prevented or mitigated had it been in use.

Of course, the Great Western ATC or ACS was not perfect. Being electro-mechanical in operation, it could fail to operate under some circumstances, and Norton Fitzwarren sadly demonstrated that it was not a complete safeguard against driver error. Even so, the GWR record in safety was almost irreproachable.

The Southern's good record was partly due to considerable extension of colour-light signalling, which by its improved visibility reduces the likelihood of a driver missing a signal. Instead of a single distant signal with a relatively weak light at night, a driver in a colour-light multiple-aspect area would receive first a conspicuous double yellow and then a single yellow before reaching a stop indication. The Southern electrification also helped, since the motorman in the front cab of an electric train has a far better view of signals than a steam locomotive driver. Lastly, the Southern greatly extended track circuiting in its re-signalling schemes.

The LNER undertook piecemeal improvements in signalling rather than major schemes, certainly at first. The replacement of semaphore distant signals by isolated colour-light signals was a useful step, and in 1933 automatic colour-light signalling was installed on the East Coast Main Line between York and Northallerton, following an earlier installation between Marylebone and Wembley replacing the semaphores and manual signal boxes as far as Neasden.

The LMS had in the Hudd electro-magnetic form of ATC on the London, Tilbury & Southend section a system that was inherently more advanced than the robust and simple GWR type. In a refined and much developed variation, it is now the standard British Railways Automatic Warning System in widespread use. So it is surprising that the LMS management took no steps to install it generally, particularly in view of the number of LMS accidents which it could have prevented. Financial stringency was not so severe as on the LNER, and when the very heavy cost of accidents – compensation for deaths and injuries, replacement or repair of loco-

Above: *The LNER's only diesel railcar,* Tyneside Venturer, *almost identical in appearance with the better-known Sentinel steam railcars* (L&GRP/David & Charles)

Below: *The LNER beaver-tail observation car of the Coronation train* (Crown copyright, National Railway Museum)

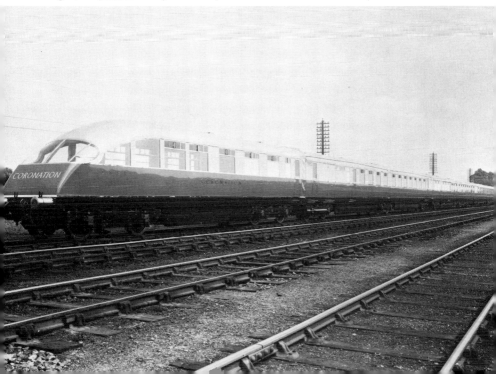

Above: *The Eastern Belle Sunday excursion Pullman train in the charge of a Sandringham 4-6-o* (British Rail)

Below: *A Robinson GC Atlantic heading a train of former LSWR stock, including a clerestory diner on the Newcastle—Bournemouth through service* (L&GRP/David & Charles)

motives, rolling stock and track and structures, delays and diversions – is taken into account, one may feel that the LMS and probably also the LNER could have justified the outlay on the biggest single requirement to improve rail safety during the lifetime of the four great railways, namely enforcing obedience to signal indications by positive means instead of relying solely on fallible human nature, however carefully trained and conscientious.

CHAPTER 9

The Railways and the Road Lorry

Economic historians often consider that the most significant feature – and railwaymen the most regrettable feature – of railway history between 1923 and 1939 was the loss of rail freight traffic to the roads. It is certain that this was the biggest single factor in the financial difficulties of the LNER and the LMS, the heaviest freight carriers. Much less has been written on whether the railways could have done more on their own account to stem the growing losses, or whether successive Governments ought to have intervened to relieve the railways of some of the restrictions which, the railways alleged, made the competition from road transport unfair and prevented them from effectively countering it.

It all really started with the 1914–18 war, in which two things happened; the Government ordered large quantities of road lorries, which had to be robust and reliable, for Army service; and it trained large numbers of servicemen (and some women) as drivers and mechanics. After the war three other things happened. Ex-servicemen trained in road transport began to look for a new career; the Government handed them a cash gratuity on demobilisation; and army surplus vehicles were put on sale in large numbers. The circumstances were ideal for the birth of a new road haulage industry based on small, competitive firms, often of owner-drivers.

Of course, before the war there had been well-established cartage and haulage firms, gradually changing from horse to motor traction. But these had mostly been used to co-operate rather than compete with the railways. Pickfords, Mutter Howey and other well-known names had acted as railway

126

cartage agents for many years and had not much in common with the new race of 'little men' who entered the industry between 1918 and around 1920.

Some of the new men went bankrupt through lack of financial experience but many survived and built up substantial businesses. They had certain advantages over the railways. They could charge what they liked, and they could go anywhere. They could pick and choose their customers and also what they would carry, whereas the railways had to accept almost anything offered to them for transport.

Lastly, and very important, the road men could walk into any railway goods office and demand to see the rate book. From it they could learn exactly what the railway would charge for any given job, and it was then a simple matter to knock whatever percentage was needed off the railway rate in order to secure the traffic. The railways had no corresponding means of ascertaining what the haulier was charging, and even if they knew it, the legal restrictions upon their charges might make it impossible to offer a competitive rate.

Of course, this is not the whole story. The haulier offered in many cases not just a cheaper but a superior service – at any rate for traffic that had to be collected and delivered by road. Transhipment at goods stations between road and rail involved risks of damage, delay and pilferage which were avoided when a road lorry gave direct door to door service. Reliability and guaranteed delivery time were potent factors in inducing traders to change to road transport. A rail wagon has no voice; if it is wrongly marshalled, or put in a cripple siding because it develops some mechanical defect, it sits there silently waiting for someone to come along and notice it. But a lorry driver is by comparison very vocal. He is virtually inseparable from his load, anxious to complete the job and go home, able to report any delay by telephone and to summon assistance in the event of a breakdown.

Of course these factors, so important in the case of rail 'c and d' (collected and delivered) traffic, did not operate so strongly in the case of 's to s' (station to station) traffic, where the sender or the recipient preferred to perform his own cartage, and still less in the case of 'ps to ps' traffic (private siding to private siding). Where rail sidings were laid into coal mines, power stations or steelworks, the convenience of bulk transit by rail was obvious, and the relatively low rates per ton charged upon, for instance, coal, iron ore and steel products in bulk continued to tie heavy industry to the use of rail.

Yet, in the inter-war years, even firms with private siding facilities for what the railways termed 'general merchandise' traffic were allowing the rail connections to become disused, while many firms building new factories (who 50 years earlier would have applied for a rail connection as a matter of course) now did not consider it necessary, their whole goods receipt and despatch arrangements being geared to road transport.

The railways certainly fought back. The LNER had a senior officer known as the Industrial Agent whose task was to persuade firms to build new factories adjacent to the railway – where possible on railway-owned land – and install a rail connection. Both the LMS and the GWR followed similar policies through their Goods Managers. But success in this campaign could be only partial in face of the strong trend towards road transport.

To some historians the railways seem to have been rather slow to observe the significance of what was happening. The statistics are pretty obvious. In 1920 only 101,000 road motor goods vehicles had been registered; by 1935 there were 435,000 – a steady rise being registered year by year. If one looks at the general merchandise carried by the four main line railways, that is, the type of freight suitable for road *or* rail transport, the tonnage was 80.8 millions in the first year after grouping, 1923, but only 65.5 millions in 1935.

The reaction of the railways to this erosion of freight traffic fell, roughly, into three phases. In the first, which lasted from

1923 to around 1927, there was a certain apathy born of confidence that the railways were going to remain the principal freight transport mode in the country. But the general strike of May 1926 produced something of a shock since it demonstrated that, even with the railways out of action, a great deal of essential traffic could be handled by road.

In the second phase, the railways began to campaign against the 'unfairness' of road competition, pointing out how restricted were the railways' powers to quote competitive rates and arguing that such a free-for-all was against the long-term national interest. The railways certainly had a point. Nineteenth-century legislation designed to protect the trading community against railway abuse of monopoly power had laid down that rates must not exceed certain maxima; that they must be published for all to see; that there could be no picking and choosing between customers and no 'unfair discrimination'. The last was very hampering because it meant that if the railways conceded a specially low rate to one trader, any other trader offering traffic under similar conditions was entitled to the reduction. So competitive rate-cutting, to keep on rail a traffic that one particular trader was threatening to give to a road haulier, might have dangerous consequences.

The railways' grievances were aired before the Royal Commission on Transport which sat from 1928 to 1930, and they had some effect in persuading the Commission to recommend the introduction of a licensing system for road transport, both buses and coaches (which happened under the Road Traffic Act of 1930) and lorries (under the Road and Rail Traffic Act of 1933). These Acts virtually froze the size of commercial road transport fleets, and the 1933 Act also gave the railways some relaxation as regards charging powers by allowing the quotation of what were known as agreed charges under which the railways could do a package deal with a trader to carry the whole of his traffic at a flat rate per ton anywhere in Great Britain – a sort of parcels post charging principle.

But the whole elaborate machinery for regulating railway charges was out of date. The 1921 Railways Act had required the railways to submit charging schemes to a judicial body created by the Act known as the Railway Rates Tribunal. These schemes were to link railway charges with profits on a sliding scale by fixing a standard revenue for each of the four great companies (in effect, the 1913 net revenues plus an allowance for subsequent capital expenditure). If the railways in any year earned more than the standard revenue, in the next year charges must be reduced by an amount calculated to absorb 80 per cent of the excess, only 20 per cent being retained by the railway company.

It was unrealistic, being based on the obsolete idea that railways were a monopoly. By 1 January 1928, the appointed day when the freight charges scheme took effect, the railways were in hot competition with the roads. In no year of the life of the four companies did they earn their standard revenue.

Apart from the endless arguments about charges by road and rail, the railways did make some efforts to match the service the road haulier could offer. Containers began to be introduced in relatively small sizes that could be carried on a standard railway collection and delivery vehicle or placed in an open wagon. Cranage was an essential part of the operation of road–rail transfer. Larger containers carried on special four-wheeled flat wagons ('Conflats') were also built. But transhipment was too slow and containers much too small in comparison with the Freightliner system developed in the 1960s.

The growth in the use of containers was possibly depressed by the surcharge made for their use, the so-called 'container differential' which the railways justified on the grounds of offering a superior service. Even so, the total number of containers in stock by 1937 had risen to 13,800. A considerable amount of furniture removal work was carried out by rail container with specialist removers such as Pickfords performing the packing and unpacking.

Damage to goods caused by rough shunting of wagons caused much dissatisfaction and heavy claims against the railways. Two expedients were adopted to reduce damage. One was the installation of rail brakes in large marshalling yards to control, with considerable precision, the speeds at which wagons ran down from the hump to buffer up and form new train sets. The other was the development of a shock-absorbing wagon (code name SHOCVAN) in which the body could slide a short distance upon the underframe, controlled by springs which absorbed much of the impact of a rough shunt. These measures, though useful, were only palliatives.

In the second phase of road–rail competition the railways began to be aware that traffic was being lost not merely to professional road hauliers, but also because large firms were increasingly using their own road transport to carry their own goods – an activity that was not at all restricted by the quantity licensing system introduced by the 1933 Act. Anyone could obtain what was known as a C licence for a vehicle to carry his own goods. Originally such vehicles had been engaged almost entirely in short-distance and distributive work, such as the milk round, the baker's round, the delivery vehicles of the department stores. But now large firms were building up substantial fleets of vehicles, often of high capacity, to fetch their raw materials, to deliver to customers, to transfer stores, spare parts and semi-finished articles between factories. The huge Unilever group built up a separate subsidiary company, SPD Ltd, solely engaged in road transport for that great conglomerate and all its operating companies.

This kind of competition was the hardest of all for the railways to match. Once a firm had invested in a fleet of road vehicles the chances of it writing off the investment and returning to the use of rail transport were minimal.

In the third phase of competition, the railways at last went over to the offensive, and used the Parliamentary powers to operate road transport obtained in 1928. They used the powers fairly cautiously. The first main move was the purchase of Hay's Wharf Cartage Co Ltd in 1930 which gave them control of the long-established road firm of Pickfords which for many years had been associated with the railways. At the same time Carter Paterson Ltd, a household word in road parcels carrying, was acquired. There were appreciable subsequent investments; for instance, the LMS acquired a half share in Wordie & Co of Glasgow and the entire share capital of Joseph Nall & Co of Manchester, a long-established haulage business.

None of this really amounted to large-scale diversification, to a substantial move away from rail to road transport; it was more like testing the water temperature with one foot. However, in 1938 the railways took, for them, a pretty bold step by launching a campaign under the name of the 'Square Deal', to persuade the Government to abolish all restrictions on railway charges and obligations to carry, justified by the argument that railways were no longer a monopoly and should be allowed to compete freely with road.

Opposition came from many quarters – predictably from the Road Haulage Association and also from various traders' associations which feared that cutting rates in some quarters would lead to raising them elsewhere. After long negotiations and discussions, however, the opposition obtained various guarantees and the Government announced that, in principle, it was prepared to concede the railways' main proposals. Before legislation could be enacted, however, 3 September 1939 dawned and the country was at war.

The war experiences of the companies will be described in a later chapter, but an immediate effect of the emergency was to restore the railways, using home-produced coal, to the position of the basic mode of transport. Fuel rationing and the end of vehicle construction for any owner other than the Government, together with a permit system for road haulage operations, utterly changed the position. From struggling to retain traffic, the railways quickly became faced with the problem of how to handle all the traffic on offer.

This position continued throughout the war and until nationalisation in 1948. So the companies, in their last years of existence, had no immediate problems from road competition. But the lessons of the 1920s and 1930s were not forgotten, and in their post-war planning the railways envisaged much more diversification and participation in road transport, though not on the lines which the Government incorporated in the Transport Act 1947. Paradoxically, if nationalisation had not been enforced, there might well have been considerably more steps towards practical integration of road and rail freight traffic, though of course on a voluntary and not a doctrinaire, statutory basis.

CHAPTER 10
The State of the Railways

Each of the four groups – with the exception of the Great Western – inherited a rather variable quality of infrastructure, parts built to high standards and well maintained, parts more cheaply built and, here and there, verging on the decrepit. The policies of the former companies had of course differed; the Great Northern had long followed the maxim of its last Chairman, Sir Frederick Banbury, that 'there is no money in stations'. The tradition that King's Cross had been built for less than the cost of the ornamental 'Propylaeum' or Doric Arch at Euston was upheld in the GNR's economy, amounting to meanness, in the layout of stations such as Peterborough, Grantham, Retford, Doncaster and Leeds (Central). On the other hand the London, Brighton & South Coast built and rebuilt many stations with wide platforms and spacious accommodation, apparently believing that where a service is to be sold, the look of the shop window is important.

No railway had a more varied collection of stations than the LMS, with the gloomy muddle of Preston and the shabby, confused dignity of Euston, the simplicity of Barlow's great Gothic train shed at St Pancras and the many clean, well designed Midland wayside stations with their fully glazed umbrella roofs. There was the classical dignity of Huddersfield (almost lost under its coat of grime), the charming pavilions designed by Francis Thompson for the North Midland Railway, the airy, spacious Caledonian stations at places such as Wemyss Bay, and the utter dreariness of so many stations in the West Midlands, Lancashire and Yorkshire.

The LNER also inherited a mixed bag. The Great Northern's penny-pinching was countered by the Great Central's outlay – which it could ill afford – on its pleasant London Extension line stations, and by the North Eastern's imposing edifices at York, Newcastle, and many other places. The Great Eastern was the possessor of a strange mixture, ranging from the spacious and modern at Felixstowe to the squalor of the Enfield and Chingford line stations. The North British, apart from Edinburgh Waverley, seemed to have grudged money on stations as much as the Great Northern, though its West Highland line demonstrated higher standards, and the little Great North of Scotland was not at all discreditable.

The Southern also came into possession of an extraordinary variety, ranging from the gloom and dirt of some places on the South Eastern's North Kent line to the spaciousness of wayside stations such as Horley or Streatham Common on the LBSC.

Policies varied even after grouping. The LMS prepared many plans for reconstruction, few of which were carried out. The LNER flirted with the idea of rebuilding King's Cross but the project never got off the ground. The Great Western, already with fewer black spots than any other company, gradually eliminated those that they had such as Taunton, through not on the scale of the Southern's reconstructions. One unique GWR feature was the proliferation of 'halts' in, for instance, the London suburban area and on the Swindon–Gloucester line, which were served by railcars or autotrains, (first steam and later diesel). They consisted of short platforms with extraordinary corrugated iron shelters of definitely Oriental character, usually known as 'pagodas'.

The LMS was afflicted with an Estate Department which seemed to see passenger stations not as shop windows for transport but solely as sites for commercial lettings. Tenants were installed wherever a plot could be let, even if this completely obscured the station entrance (as at Kilburn High Road), or made architectural nonsense of an otherwise well-planned building. All the companies of course experienced the need to raise revenue from this source, but the LMS seemed more ruthless than the others in its pursuit of rentals.

As regards the preservation of buildings of architectural merit, on the whole the tale is sad. The 1920s and 1930s were decades when 19th century architecture was automatically decried; to label a building as 'Victorian' was to imply that it was ripe for demolition and replacement. It was an age that saw Nash's Regent Street replaced by the stodgy mock-Renaissance blocks that we dislike so much to-day, and an age that allowed that crowning act of vandalism, the pulling down of Adam's exquisite Adelphi Terrace facing the Thames and its replacement with a hideous office block. So perhaps the railways cannot be blamed for not having better taste than the rest of contemporary society or contemporary Governments. But there are instances all over the country of stations built by architects of considerable sensibility, well adapted to their original purpose and blending well with their surroundings, that were butchered by successive District Engineers. Windows bricked up, extensions in unsuitable materials, new verandah roofs completely out of scale, and a general hotch-potch of tinkering that completely ignored the original design, were too often the cause of virtual obliteration of an admirable concept. Part of the trouble lay in the organisation. On the railways the Architect generally was subordinate to the Chief Engineer, and was too often regarded by that potentate as someone whose function was, now and again, to apply cosmetic treatment to structures whose basic design was an engineering matter.

The LMS allowed Euston to become an ever-greater muddle, the splendid Great Hall being cluttered up with timber partitions to make enquiry offices known to the staff as 'Follows's folly'; it let Gilbert Scott's triumphal apotheosis of the Gothic in the St Pancras Hotel be first neglected and then knocked about for conversion into (very unsatisfactory) office suites. The LNER allowed Cubitt's simple and dignified King's Cross to be ruined by a huddle of shabby one-storey buildings in front, generally known as the 'African Village'.

136

Examples of this insensitivity can be found all over the country.

There were, however, a few creditable exceptions. The Southern's new concrete stations can best be described as belonging to the Jazz Age, but they were at least efficient for their purpose. The LNER built a few workmanlike new stations in brick, of which Berwick-on-Tweed is a particularly good example; others included Clacton-on-Sea, and several wayside stations between York and Northallerton.

Economy, or rather the need to show economy, was a main cause of unsatisfactory maintenance and cleanliness at many stations, though over-rigid departmental organisation played its part. Stationmasters were not allowed to arrange for minor repairs with a local contractor, but had to submit requests through their superior for transmission to the appropriate department – the Chief Engineer's or the Chief Mechanical Engineer's – where delays of weeks or months might elapse before a broken window was repaired or an electrical fitting replaced.

An exceptional railwayman, who believed that tidiness and order around the tracks gave an impression of efficiency and helped to maintain a high morale, was John Miller, Civil Engineer of the North Eastern Area of the LNER. He carried out many improvements to the structures entrusted to his department and in particular initiated the systematic cleaning up of areas adjoining the tracks which on too many railways were allowed to become waste land or rubbish dumps. He laid out grass plots with neat concrete edgings at junctions and though he sometimes had to resort to unorthodox expedients to finance his many improvements, he was a pioneer of railway 'good housekeeping', a field in which, unfortunately, too many railway officers took little interest.

It must however be stressed that all four groups, whatever their policy on stations and tidiness, maintained their 'safety structures' – bridges, viaducts, tunnels and so on – to high standards. The Chief Engineers, who had to sign an annual certificate for the Board and the shareholders that the Company's infrastructure had been properly maintained, were not denied the funds to meet this obligation.* Economy certainly delayed some desirable works for a time, for example, the strengthening of some bridges on the Midland main line to enable more powerful locomotives to be used and thereby overcoming the uneconomic persistent double-heading. But it was not allowed to affect essentials; Chief Engineers were autocrats wherever safety was involved.

In permanent way, too, standards were not merely preserved but, in the case of routes inherited from some of the constituent companies, raised. The LNWR had formerly illustrated its track in a poster claiming that the company had the best permanent way in the world. The Midland had used the slogan 'The Best Way', which the LMS later adopted as its own.

For a long time change in track design was slow. The 45ft standard rail gradually gave way to the 60ft rail which as early as 1894 the LNWR had begun to roll in its own steel mill at Crewe. Bull-head rails, held in cast-iron chairs by oak keys, with the chairs secured by coach screws rather than spikes, continued to be the standard, though in the early 1930s the first lengths of flat-bottomed rail were laid in the Midland main line near London, and other experimental lengths followed. There was an extended trial of two-hole fishplates for joining the rail-ends in place of the traditional four-hole type, but eventually there was a reversion to the older pattern which proved stronger.

On the Southern extensive use was made of the 'Ellson joint', named after George Ellson, the Southern's Chief Engineer who had designed it. This was an attempt to reduce rail-joint shocks to wheels and suspension – the familiar 'clickety-click' – and also to prevent dropped joints in the track. It substituted for the simple butt-joint a rail-end

---

* The LNER auditors on occasion had reservations about the adequacy of the maintenance provisions.

machined in an S-curve, the wheels being supported by both rails as they passed over the joint and the fishplate bolts of course passing through both rails. The Ellson joint was costly, involving accurate machining of the rail-ends to the S-profile, and was eventually discarded. Today, continuous welding of rail lengths achieves the same object much more simply and cheaply.

Apart from rebuilding and major engineering works, how did the four groups look after their inheritance? Sadly, one must conclude that good housekeeping and routine mainte-nance tended to suffer with the greater size, greater imperson-ality and possibly reduced staff morale on both the LMS and the LNER. Things were rather better on the Great Western and the Southern, mainly because they were smaller and hence more manageable, and the boss's eye was not so far away.

Economy was practised most systematically by the LMS. Sometimes it undoubtedly led to greater efficiency; sometimes a deterioration in service quality seemed to result. In motive power the LMS rationalised the use of steam locomotives with considerable effect. Between 1923 and 1939 it built about 3,500 new locomotives, but reduced the locomotive stock (10,300 at the grouping) by over 2,500 units. (In this, changes to electric or diesel traction played only an insignifi-cant part.) Units under or awaiting repair in 1937 were only one-fifth of the number in 1923. Yet both train-miles per-formed and the average speed of passenger trains had sub-stantially increased during the period.

This achievement was impressive. It was not of course solely the result of mechanical engineering reforms, but also of a new operating philosophy, that of maximum utilisation within the limits imposed by the characteristics of the steam locomotive, such as the need to take in water and coal, and to clean the fire and smokebox, as well as the firetubes, at fairly frequent intervals. It involved cyclic diagramming of locomo-tives under which a complicated series of duties might be performed by an engine before it returned to its home depot, in the course of which it might be handled by several crews. Conversely, enginemen might handle a considerable number of different locomotives in the course of working a weekly diagram.

Of course, the day had long passed when drivers and firemen could be allocated to a single engine, as when in William Stroudley's day on the LBSCR the driver's name was painted in the cab. In those more leisurely times, when enginemen worked a 12-hour day, a driver's ability to speak, often with pride, of 'my engine' certainly had some advantages. Since every steam locomotive is individual, even if slightly so, in handling characteristics, an intimate knowledge of engine on the part of both driver and fireman certainly helped to maintain standards of performance. A driver also would be insistent in checking that repairs had been properly carried out on 'his' engine, whereas at the end of a turn on a locomotive that he might not drive again for a considerable time, faults might be left for the next crew to experience and report.

Cyclic diagramming also meant, all too often, that locomotives were not cleaned as they should be. Splendid though Stanier's Princess and Coronation Pacifics usually looked, many less glamorous locomotive types were too often seen in filthy condition on the LMS.

On the other railways the drive for high utilisation was not pushed quite so ruthlessly. On the LNER attempts were made at times to limit the number of crews assigned to drive any one engine and thus retain some of the traditional relationship between locomotives and the men on the footplate. On the GWR, footplate men had always been an aristocracy, enjoying pension fund privileges, for example, and this tradition long survived. Top link men at major sheds were more specialised, more confined to a narrow range of duties than on the LMS with its cyclic diagramming. On the Southern the shorter distances and the progressive contraction in the use of

Above: *One of the Southern's modern station exteriors at Chessington South. (The vintage horsebus was for visitors to Chessington Zoo)* (L&GRP/David & Charles)

Below: *The Sunny South Express through train from Liverpool and Manchester to the South Coast at Addison Road on the West London Railway, with LMS coaches headed by a Marsh Atlantic in SR colours* (L&GRP/David & Charles)

Above: *Perhaps the most individual of all the Joint lines: a through train on the M&GN, with both Midland and Great Northern characteristics very obvious* (L&GRP/David & Charles)

Below: *A tiny enclave: a train on the Dundalk, Newry, and Greenore section of the LMS. The Crewe influence is very apparent* (L&GRP/David & Charles)

steam power were over-riding factors.

An observer of the railways, looking at standards of maintenance including cleanliness of stations as well as that of locomotives and rolling stock, would probably not have found
very much to criticise on the Great Western or the Southern
before war conditions spread their blight everywhere. On the
two great northern companies the picture is more of a patch-
work. On parts of the systems – particularly perhaps in
Scotland – old standards and old traditions survived surprisingly well. Elsewhere, here and there the grouping seemed to
have depressed the pride and morale of management, perhaps
because a clear-cut entity was submerged into a larger, more
impersonal one.

If the shape of the railways did not change very greatly, this
was largely due to shortage of funds for investment. The railways' financial performance was not one that made it easy to
raise capital by issuing new stock. But with the example of the
Southern, one may feel that more electrification could and
should have been carried out (if Herbert Walker's strict
control over outlays could have been observed) on both the
LMS and the LNER, particularly in the case of the latter's
London suburban services.

But in 1935 the Government at last provided finance at low
rates of interest for railway investment, in order to relieve
unemployment and to stimulate the economy generally.
Through a Railway Finance Corporation, £30 million was
made available for what became known as the New Works
Programme, 1935–40. Under it the GWR proposed to build a
new line from near St Germans in Cornwall to Looe, a
distance of seven miles, greatly shortening the roundabout
route via Liskeard, and a diversion between Dawlish Warren
and Newton Abbot, 8½ miles long. The Southern Railway
agreed to extend its electrified mileage by taking advantage of
the low-interest finance now offered, carrying the third rail
from Hampton Court Junction (near Surbiton) to Portsmouth, from West Worthing to Havant, and from Dorking to

Arundel Junction, together with several shorter sections. On the South Eastern side electrification was to be carried to Chatham and Gillingham, and from Strood to Maidstone (West).

The LMS agreed to electrify the lines of the former Wirral Railway which it had taken over at the grouping, while the LNER proposed electrification of the Manchester–Sheffield–Wath line of the former Great Central Railway, the heavily-used trans-Pennine route for coal traffic, on the 1,500 volts d.c. overhead system, which incidentally in 1931 had been recommended by a Government committee (the Pringle Committee) as the standard for future main line electrification in Britain.

Some of the works included in the programme were never carried out and some had to wait for completion until long after nationalisation. The outbreak of war in 1939 was the proximate cause of delay or abandonment of schemes which included, on the LMS, the rebuilding of Euston, and much extension of colour-light signalling, and on the LNER, doubling of single lines to Felixstowe and Clacton, colour-light signalling at various places and building of new locomotives and rolling stock. The Great Western had an ambitious list of stations to be modernised, including Exeter (St David's) and Plymouth (North Road).

In the same year, 1935, the Government announced a similar plan for suburban railway electrification and tube extension in the London area, with finance being made available, again at low interest rates, up to £35 million.

Although London Transport was to be the main recipient, the LNER participated to the extent of proposing to electrify between Liverpool Street and Shenfield. It was also planned that the Central Line of London Transport should be extended westwards over the Great Western as far as West Ruislip and possibly Denham; and eastwards, partly in tube tunnel, to join with the former Loughton/Epping/Ongar and Hainault Loop lines of the Great Eastern section. This was

144

intended to relieve pressure on Liverpool Street at peak hours. A similar projection of the Northern line over the Great Northern branches from Finsbury Park to Edgware, High Barnet and Alexandra Palace recalls the old Great Northern Railway Company's efforts to rid itself of the 'suburban incubus' many years ago.

The completion of these works, delayed by the war, did not take place until after nationalisation, and the original proposals were modified in various ways. The Alexandra Palace branch was omitted from the electrification and eventually closed, the Edgware line was cut back to Mill Hill East, and the Central Line westward extension did not get beyond West Ruislip.

As a counterpart to the enquiry into how the companies looked after the assets they acquired at the grouping, there is of course the question whether they should not have discarded many more of these assets as unprofitable. The Beeching studies, 15 years after nationalisation, shocked many people by disclosing how large a proportion of the railway mileage open for traffic was and had for a long time been hopelessly uneconomic.

Between 1923 and 1938 the four companies showed in their statistics a *net* reduction of 307 route-miles open for traffic. The actual mileage closed was somewhat greater, because some short lengths of new railway were opened in these years. By and large, however, it is clear that the total system at the outbreak of the second world war was in essence the same as it had been fifteen years earlier, at the grouping. The economic consequences of maintaining such a large infrastructure, parts of which we now know were unable to operate profitably, will be evident in Chapter 14.

CHAPTER 11
The Railwaymen

By the time the four groups came into existence the great battles that had been fought by the unions to secure recognition from the companies for negotiation on wages and conditions of service, and to establish an agreed machinery of conciliation to resolve disputes, had passed into history. The National Union of Railwaymen (succeeding the former Amalgamated Society of Railway Servants), the Associated Society of Locomotive Engineers and Firemen, and the Railway Clerks Association, were all well established by 1923, with a total membership of around 500,000. The first-named was an industrial union embracing all grades; the second was a craft union representing a group of skilled workers; and the third was a white-collar union representing the clerical staff below management level. The workshop staff were separately organised in the appropriate engineering unions.

The North Eastern Railway in 1897 had been the first to recognise a union, the ASRS. From that time until the first world war, there had been a good deal of unrest among railwaymen, partly because of rising prices which eroded the real value of money wages, and partly the growth of what was termed the New Unionism, more militant than the original movement and with political affiliations.

In 1906 the ASRS had drawn up a national all-grades proposal for improved wages which, being rejected by the companies, had led to a strike threat. The strike was only averted by the conciliation efforts of Lloyd George, then President of the Board of Trade. In 1911 there was a series of local railwaymen's strikes, mainly in the North of England. During the 1914–18 war, strikes were prevented by emergency legislation and by concessions which the Government instructed the companies to make. But in 1919 there was a national railway strike, ended by Government intervention (the railways still being under Government control) which led to a settlement.

By the time the railways were grouped it was firm Government policy that there must be a statutory machinery for settling disputes. Conciliation Boards for each railway had been devised by Lloyd George and amended in 1911; they were replaced in 1919, following the strike in that year, by a Central Wages Board and a National Wages Board to deal with all wages questions, the railways being required to act in unison.

The Central Wages Board was composed of equal numbers of management and union representatives. Should it fail to reach agreement, matters were referred to the National Wages Board, which had four representatives of the companies, four from the unions, and four of railway users, plus an independent chairman.

The Railways Act 1921 revised the constitution of the Central and National Wages Boards, enlarging their membership, and it also provided for the preparation of schemes, which were to be agreed between the companies and the unions, for more detailed machinery for settling disputes. The schemes eventually agreed provided for Local Departmental Committees (LDCs) at any station or depot where more than 75 staff were employed, and for five Sectional Councils on each main line railway, covering the main groups of workers. A Railway Council was also to be appointed for each railway, the union side of which would comprise members of the Sectional Councils.

Thereafter it was often said that the railways had a more comprehensive machinery for maintaining labour relations than almost any other industry. Certainly the stormy years from the turn of the century to the outbreak of war in 1914 were succeeded between the two wars by greater stability, for which two factors were largely responsible. First, the fall in the price level over much of the period enhanced the real value of earnings. The formidable level of unemployment, too, meant that a relatively secure job such as one on the railways was something to value. And the new conciliation machinery worked pretty well, with representatives of staff and of management getting to know each other round the meeting table.

It is important to remember that the companies' side acted in complete unison on personnel matters, through two bodies, the Railway Companies Association and the Railways Staff Conference. The former was a body of some antiquity, founded as the 'United Railway Companies Committee' as early as 1856, becoming the Railway.Companies Association in 1869. Its main function was to co-ordinate and assist the interests of the railways – in essence, those of the shareholders – in Parliament. It was in fact quite an effective railway lobby. After 1923 it also ensured that the railway companies preserved a unified front in labour relations, the executive work being entrusted to the chief officers for personnel comprising the Railways Staff Conference.

The major crises in labour relations were the general strike in May 1926 and the reduction in wages between 1928 and 1930, and again between 1931 and 1937. In these instances, all three unions followed the same policy. But before then, in 1924 the Associated Society of Locomotive Engineers and Firemen had called a strike on account of an award by the National Wages Board which the NUR had accepted. ASLEF objected particularly to the raising of the datum line for mileage bonus payments to footplatemen from 120 to 150 miles per day. Since those footplatemen who were NUR members – rather less than half the number in ASLEF – mostly continued to work, the bitterness between the two unions was considerable. The ASLEF strike lasted from 21 to 29 January, and achieved little except a staging and partial postponement of the new procedures. It left inter-union relations considerably soured for a long time.

Far more important, however, was the support given to the miners by all three railway unions in the general strike from 3 to 12 May, 1926. There was an almost complete withdrawal of labour by the wages grades, but rather less complete by the salaried staff who were members of the Railway Clerks Association.

There is considerable folk-lore regarding the volunteers who were recruited by the companies and who seized the opportunity to enjoy themselves on the railway while also convinced that they were acting patriotically. Students and middle-aged men alike jumped at the chance of driving a locomotive or manning a signalbox; some brought to the tasks a considerable amateur knowledge of railways as well as enthusiasm. But the most general image was one of young men in plus-fours – that curious garment originally a uniform for golfers but later a badge of upper-middle-class origin – and sweaters, light-heartedly making mistakes that in most cases had no serious consequences. Professor Bagwell in *The Railwaymen* has quoted a story told by the Chairman of the GWR about a volunteer at Paddington for whom work could not at first be found. 'He willingly accepted the task of oiling the points all along the line. He was provided with a can of oil, and then nothing was heard of him for three whole days. On the fourth day, a telegram was received at headquarters from him. It came from Bristol and read: "Please send me some more oil!"'

Accidents were few, because trains were few, and proceeded with extreme caution from signalbox to signalbox. But day by day the number of trains crept up, partly through volunteer activity, partly through strikers drifting back to work. Violence by strikers against the volunteers was fortunately not very common, despite a few unpleasant incidents. The most serious case, in which a train from Edinburgh to London was derailed by a rail having been removed from the track, was not the action of railwaymen, but of a group of miners, who were indicted and punished by sentences of imprisonment for between four and eight years.

The railway strike collapsed, anticipating the end of the general strike, on 12 May. The blow to trade unionism was severe, and the railway companies were quick to announce that reinstatement of men on strike would not be automatic. The damage done by the strike meant that less work in total was available and short-time working and unemployment followed in some areas until matters returned more or less to normal. Action taken during the strike was also entered on each man's staff record, and in the case of clerical staff loyalty in 1926 was a factor often taken into account when promotion was in question later on. Following the return to work, the companies and the unions also agreed that in future the machinery of conciliation would always be utilised.

The dislocation of the general strike had faded when in July 1928 the companies presented to the unions a case for a general reduction in wages, based upon the deterioration in the financial position of the railways. Eventually a reduction of 2½ per cent across the board, applying to everyone from directors to starting grade employees, was agreed, to begin in August 1929. The cut, however, was not long-lived and wage levels were restored in May 1930.

But the world-wide economic blizzard again put railway finances in a very serious position, and in 1931 the National Wages Board authorised a reduction of 2½ per cent overall, with a further 2½ per cent deduction from wages over 40s per week or salaries of over £100 per annum, to operate from March 1931.

When the national economy had made a recovery, the cuts were reversed, first of all in 1934 by eliminating the second 2½ per cent and then in 1936 by getting rid of the basic 2½ per cent in two instalments of 1¼ per cent each, in August 1936 and August 1937.

If one asks whether railway policy in personnel matters was enlightened and progressive during the inter-war years, no easy answer appears. By the standards of the time, the railways were good but not model employers. Pay was not high, and staff were often keen to enhance it by extra work such as fogmen's duties, rest day working or extra mileage payments. Job security was good, but discipline was still strict and cautions, suspensions, downgrading, or in the last instance dismissal, were firmly applied for any breach. The companies had no official pensions scheme for wages staff – the 'Company's servants', in the time-honoured Victorian phrase – though there were numerous mutual societies, in some cases assisted by the company, under which sick benefits and pensions, albeit on a small scale, were provided. The Great Western was particularly good in this respect, and staff welfare was watched over with a more paternal interest than on any other company.

The Railway Convalescent Homes and the Railway Benevolent Institution were also major welfare activities which, though nominally independent charitable organisations, were helped by the companies in various ways.

Criticism can be levelled at the absence of really systematic vocational training facilities, and the rather basic tests of knowledge and aptitude for those eligible for promotion. Signalmen were tested in their knowledge of block working, of the rule book, and of local rules applying to the box in which they were to work, by Signalmen's Inspectors. Similarly, firemen were passed for driving on their knowledge of the locomotive and of the rule book by Locomotive Inspectors. Knowledge of the routes over which they worked, especially the signals, could be obtained by special route-learning journeys; but it was – and still is – generally left to the driver to satisfy himself that his route knowledge was adequate. Of course, in most cases drivers had had many years of working over the routes as firemen.

In general, training was given rather by rule of thumb, on the job, though there were some signalling schools and enginemen's Mutual Improvement Classes, as well as classes for gangers and inspectors organised by the Permanent Way

Institution. For the clerical grades there were classes at main centres in such subjects as Goods and Passenger Stations Accounts. All these classes were held in the men's own time. But although the total training effort was quite considerable, it was not systematic or standardised, nor were proficiency tests as a prerequisite for promotion applied as thoroughly as was done on, for instance, many Continental railways. Promotion, in fact, below managerial level, was strongly though not exclusively based on seniority. It was expected to be given to the 'senior suitable' applicant, and, particularly in the wages grades, 'suitability' was often interpreted in a negative rather than a positive way, so that the senior man would get the post unless it could be demonstrated that he was hopelessly unsuitable. Seniority was of course always the sole criterion favoured by the unions.

For those likely to reach supervisory or middle management positions, educational and training facilities began to be established at residential schools – on the LMS at Derby, and the Southern at Woking, while the LNER set up all-line commercial and operating schools at Faverdale and Darlington respectively.

Management posts were still mainly filled by promotion from the clerical grades. As the starting grade for school leavers entering the service, as well as for adult entrants, was Class 5, the progression upwards to Class 1 and then into Special Class was a long pilgrimage and most never achieved the upper grades. Special Class clerks had the privilege of first class travel and were the grade from which managers were chiefly recruited.

From the constituent companies the grouped railways inherited various schemes of accelerated promotion for men of special ability, under the names of cadets, higher grade clerks or traffic apprentices. The LNER scheme for university graduate recruitment and training was later followed, though not so systematically nor by any means on such a scale, by the three other main lines.

To generalise about the quality of railway management is difficult. Generally there was great loyalty to the company and not many railway officers left the service. Those who did were usually tempted away by higher salaries in industry, which is itself a testimonial to their quality. The similarity with the armed services that was noteworthy in the early days of railways, when so many ex-naval or army officers had been brought in to organise the infant railway systems, was slow to disappear. The term 'officer' was often preferred to 'manager'; luncheon rooms were 'messes'. Job security and pension rights anchored many to the railway but, in the majority of cases, so did the interest of the work. 'Once a railwayman, always a railwayman' has a great deal of truth in it.

In such an atmosphere, conservatism, a liking for the established ways, can be expected to flourish. It is therefore perhaps creditable that so much innovation, as described in other chapters, took place.

A labour-intensive service industry, such as railways, is dependent upon human factors to an extent difficult to exaggerate. On the whole, and despite occasional instances of unimaginative bureaucracy and poor staff morale, the companies could claim to possess a responsible labour force and a management at least as progressive as that in British industry generally between the wars – probably better.

CHAPTER 12
The Four Great Conglomerates

One feature that has always distinguished the railways of Britain from those in most other countries has been the extent of their involvement in activities other than merely running trains. Our railways for the most part manufactured and repaired their own steam locomotives and rolling stock, operated shipping services, and have been heavily involved in hotel management as well as the catering at stations and on trains. And road transport, for the collection and delivery of goods between rail goods depots, consignors and consignees, was very widely carried on by the railways themselves, rather than by specialist road carrying firms as in other countries.

Why did the railways extend their activities so widely? After all, there had long existed in Great Britain a substantial locomotive, carriage, and wagon building industry, largely concerned with the export trade, which from time to time supplied the home railways, and would have been happy to meet their entire needs. There were plenty of shipping lines willing to co-operate with the railways, and no shortage of hotel companies and catering contractors.

The reasons were a mixed bag, and the railways did not all follow identical policies. There was probably some empire-building in the larger companies, and also a desire to be as self-sufficient as possible so that no outside supplier would be in a position to overcharge the railway or leave it short of essential requirements. There was a feeling, too, that running trains was only part of a comprehensive service which involved the provision of food and drink for passengers, and door-to-door collection and delivery for goods. Equally, shipping services were seen as essential projections of train services, linking up with other railways 'over the water'.

In the field of manufacture and repair, the groups inherited a large number of establishments but did not undertake any very drastic rationalisation. The chief reorganisation was to concentrate new building at the larger plants and devote the smaller ones to repair work. The LMS for instance found Plaistow works of the former London, Tilbury & Southend Railway (Midland) and the nearby Bow works of the former North London Railway (LNWR) were undertaking very similar work. Bow was better sited and equipped, so it was developed while Plaistow was run down. But Crewe and Derby continued as main works for new construction, just as did Doncaster and Darlington on the LNER. It was a grievance of the private manufacturers that their home orders came mainly from the very small railways and from industrial firms, unless the big railways happened temporarily to be short of capacity in their own shops. They felt that their competitors in export markets – whether the America nor the European builders of locomotives – had an advantage in the steady flow of orders from their national railway systems.

But the railway towns such as Crewe and Swindon, Derby and Doncaster even little Inverurie in Scotland – had been established so long that closing the railway works seemed unthinkable.

The railways' involvement in road collection and delivery services also had a long history. The earliest railway companies did not generally act as carriers, merely providing wagons and haulage, and leaving such firms as Pickfords or Chaplin & Horne to make the contract with the consignor and to do the cartage. Indeed, Pickfords' association with the London & Birmingham Railway was so close that for a time the firm even managed the London goods terminal of the railway at Camden.

Then the railways became restive (or perhaps over-ambitious) and decided to undertake the carriers' role themselves, displacing the cartage firms. This was, however, by no means universal, especially in the North East, the South West and Scotland, so that at the grouping in addition to railway-owned cartage there were appointed cartage firms such as Pickfords, Wordies, and Mutter Howey, maintaining a long-standing association with the railways.

But railway cartage fleets grew steadily and in 1923 no fewer than 18,000 cartage horses were owned by the four companies, as well as 32,000 horse wagons and carts, though there were only 2,000 motor goods vehicles. By the date of nationalisation the horses had fallen to 9,000, the horse wagons to 25,000, while road motors had risen to 11,000.

The survival of so much horse transport until the second half of the twentieth century is surprising at first sight. Reasons are to be found in the design of many goods stations, where the ability of the horse vehicle to turn in a very small space was essential – it led, in fact, during mechanisation, to the development of the three-wheeled tractors known as 'mechanical horses'. Other factors were the short radius of deliveries by road from goods stations spaced closely together, and the intermittent character of the work, geared as it was to the arrival or departure of freight trains.

The road collection and delivery services always operated at an accounting loss and when, long after nationalisation, it was decided to take these operations away from the railway and put them under the National Freight Corporation, the road operators discovered that the work done by railway cartage fleets, in terms of vehicle-miles per day and tons handled per day, was quite uneconomic considered purely as a road haulage operation. But it was seen by the railway companies as simply one component in a transport operation, in which one should not attempt to cost separately the rail and road portions of the journey.

If the economics of road collection and delivery were tricky, one may wonder whether the railways paid sufficient attention to the potentialities of the road passenger business.

Shortly after nationalisation, a senior officer of the former Great Western Railway joined the staff of the British Transport Commission. His new chief told him that in future he would be expected to think in transport and not purely railway terms. He replied with some acidity that the Company from which he came had thought along these lines for many years. Now it was certainly the case that the GWR had been a pioneer in operating motor bus services, that from Helston to the Lizard having been inaugurated in 1903 and followed by a number of others. Combined rail and road services such as that between London and Cheltenham had also been established.

Several other pre-grouping railways, including the LNWR and the GER, had operated motor bus services. (The SER had even operated a horse tramway along the road between Hythe and Sandgate). But after the grouping the absence of statutory powers had inhibited any development by the main line railways until new road powers were obtained from Parliament in 1928. Some fears were expressed that this might lead to a road-rail monopoly; to allay them the companies promised not to acquire a controlling interest in any road passenger business. Once the Acts had been passed, however, the railways moved quickly and as early as 1932 had invested £9½ millions in bus companies, normally through purchasing a 49 per cent or a 50 per cent interest in no less than 33 bus and coach companies belonging to the Tilling, BET and Scottish Motor Traction groups. Occasionally a more complex ownership pattern existed and the railway share was smaller; in both Sheffield and Halifax a Joint Omnibus Committee comprising the LMS, the LNER and the City Corporation operated the bus services. Railway officers joined the boards of the bus companies and the association continued until it was broken up after nationalisation.

Critics have said that this policy did not produce much in the way of road and rail co-ordination, for instance through inter-availability of tickets, or better road/rail interchange

157

arrangements, still less in the replacement of uneconomic railway services by buses. Certainly progress was far from spectacular, but some useful work was done behind the scenes by the railway members of the bus company boards. By and large, however, the railway companies regarded their investment in the bus industry mainly as a hedge against bus encroachments into rail revenues; Southern Railway officers were in fact told by their General Manager that when sitting on bus company boards they were to think as busmen, not as railwaymen. This did not stop the railways from entering objections before the Traffic Commissioners against applications by railway-associated bus companies to run extra long-distance coach services, if these were considered to compete with the trains!

On the freight side, the 1928 powers did not lead to such large-scale investment. The main feature of railway policy was the purchase in 1933 of a controlling interest in two of the largest road carriers, both long associated with the railways, Carter Paterson and Pickfords. Road haulage of course tended to be organised very differently from the bus industry. It was not dominated by large financial groups and the typical firm was small. Acquisition and control by the railways thus presented problems as well as possibilities. By the outbreak of war in 1939, however, the railways had invested in a small number of haulage businesses and seemed set to continue the process. The LMS had already a 51 per cent interest in Wordies; the LNER had inherited from the North British Railway a 49 per cent interest in Mutter Howey. But there were few signs of any policy to integrate or co-ordinate road and rail freight services.

The railways' activity as shipowners dates back almost to the earliest days. On the Clyde, where the first commercial steamer had run in 1802, the Caledonian Railway was involved as early as 1852. By 1862 the LSWR, the South Eastern and the London, Chatham & Dover were all concerned in providing cross-Channel shipping services, some-

Above: *When the Southern's Continental services still had some glamour: the Golden Arrow leaves Victoria shortly before nationalisation* (Crown copyright, National Railway Museum)

Below: *Another of the Southern's Pullmans, the Bournemouth Belle near Brockenhurst headed by* Lord Nelson *in person* (L&GRP/David & Charles)

Above: *Bulleid's Ugly Duckling: the Q1 0-6-0 freight utility locomotive built during the second world war* (Crown copyright, National Railway Museum)

Below: *A rake of Southern main line electric stock on the Brighton line, complete with Pullman* (L&GRP/David & Charles)

times through contractors or associated companies until Parliamentary powers were obtained for the railways to operate ships directly. The Great Western obtained powers to sail to the Channel Isles, to Brittany and to Ireland in 1864. The northern main lines were also involved, with the notable exception of the Great Northern Railway. The LNWR, the L&Y, the Great Central, the Midland and the North Eastern were all important operators, while the Great Eastern had been sailing from Harwich to Holland from 1863.

The organisations varied, due to both commercial and national considerations. The LBSCR steamer service between Newhaven and Dieppe was jointly owned with the Chemin de fer de l'Ouest (later the Etat) of France. The North Eastern services across the North Sea were partly joint with Humber shipping companies, partly joint with the Lancashire & Yorkshire Railway.

There is a considerable folk lore surrounding the Clyde services and the beautiful paddle-steamers owned by the Caledonian Steam Packet Company, the Glasgow & South Western and the North British Railways. The rivalry (and the racing) between the ships (including those of the independent owners) serving the islands and the lochs of the western approaches to the Clyde have passed into history.

This complex of services meant that in 1923 the railways inherited four large shipping fleets. The Southern for instance took over 21 ships of over 250 net registered tons. Ten years later, in 1933, the number had grown to 33 ships, and the total tonnage from 12,059 to 20,170. Each company developed its shipping services energetically, though some rationalisation of routes took place. For instance, in 1928 the former LNWR and L&Y joint service from Fleetwood to Belfast was transferred to Heysham and merged with the former Midland Railway service from that port. And in 1935 the LMS and LNER, with outside interests – notably Ellerman's Wilson Line – formed a joint management group, Associated Humber Lines, to operate all the shipping services of the two

161

railways based in Hull, Grimsby and Goole. If capital was short for investment in rail facilities, that did not appear to be the case on the marine side. The fleets were regularly renewed; they embodied modern marine technology and there was great pride in them. They were also for the most part profitable, though there were some, such as the services from Southampton to French ports and the Channel Islands, that had doubtful economics, though they protected the Southern's western flank from competition. Overall, the railways considered their Continental and Irish shipping services and the connecting boat trains to be jewels in their crowns; as such they were cherished.

It must be remembered that each railway was also a major dock owner. After nationalisation, when the railway docks, other than those classed as packet ports chiefly concerned with railway steamer services, were placed under the separate management of the Docks & Inland Waterways Executive, it could be seen that they fell into several geographical groups. There were those in the Humber group including Hull (ex-NER and ex-Hull & Barnsley), Goole (ex-L&YR) and Grimsby, with those in the North East – Hartlepool, Tyne, and Middlesborough docks (ex-NER) – as well as Immingham (ex-GCR). There was the important group of South Wales ports, above all those owned originally and developed by the South Wales coal lines. Southampton was a great ocean port on its own. Lastly there was a group of ports in Scotland, mainly on the Firth of Forth and built for the coal export trade.

These 'trade harbours' were built or acquired by the railways because the carriage of exports and imports by rail was a profitable part of the freight business, the traffic generally moving in sufficient volume to make it very attractive. The 'packet ports' on the other hand – Folkestone, Newhaven, Fishguard, Heysham, Holyhead, Stranraer, and Harwich (Parkeston Quay), for instance – were primarily maintained for the passenger ship business, though from a

162

number of them the railways also operated cargo vessels.

The railway-owned docks comprised a substantial proportion of the nation's port facilities, providing quays with a total length of over 500,000 ft, or say about 100 miles. But they were not very lucrative in relation to the total capital expenditure of £70 millions. Immediately before the second world war, the railways published accounts showed that the Southern Railway made a profit of £337,000 on its docks and harbours; the GWR a profit of £202,000; the LMS a small loss of £25,000; and the LNER a profit of £83,000. There was always a certain amount of controversy over the way in which receipts and expenditure were apportioned between the railway operations and the dock operations. There was scope for variations in practice which made the dock figures in isolation rather artificial. So, although the companies invested a certain amount in dock and harbour improvements – above all, the Southern at Southampton – they were subject to a good deal of criticism both from shipowners and from bodies of traders, who argued that the docks, as vital links in the country's international trade, ought not to be subservient to the interest of the railway. Only the GWR and the SR had chief officers for docks reporting directly to the General Manager, with some semblance of independence.

The railways also inherited what, to them, was an unwelcome legacy of canals. These had been acquired at various times, often as part of a bargain with the opposition in the early days when Parliamentary powers were being sought. The railways have been castigated for their failure to maintain the canals properly. But this is understandable when one observes that over the six years 1933 to 1938 inclusive, the total railway receipts from their canals varied between £168,000 and £177,000, but the expenditure, mainly on maintenance, exceeded these sums by amounts varying between £66,000 and £85,000. The railways resented having to meet such deficits and grudged the maintenance costs of the waterways.

The railways' progress towards becoming transport businesses in the widest sense moved sharply forward when in 1929 the four companies obtained Parliamentary powers to operate air services. There was considerable variation in the way in which these powers were exercised.

The LNER showed relatively little interest, partly because air competition with its chief trunk routes such as the East Coast Main Line had not appeared, partly because there were few circuitous rail journeys on its system where direct flights would show to advantage.

The other companies were more actively committed. The Southern scented a possible future impact from air upon its Continental, Channel Islands and Isle of Wight shipping services. The Great Western saw possibilities in overwater links, such as Plymouth–Cardiff, where the rail journey was very long and circuitous. The LMS was similarly interested in the Glasgow–Belfast route.

Originally the policy was to charter services from Imperial Airways. However certain independent operators were active on routes in which the railways were particularly interested, such as that to the Channel Islands. Eventually the railways combined their activities by forming in 1934 a joint subsidiary operating company in which Imperial Airways (and later also Coast Lines) participated, known as Railway Air Services. RAS took over the GWR route between Birmingham, Cardiff and Plymouth and extended it to Liverpool. Another route initiated by RAS was Liverpool–Birmingham–Bristol–Southampton–Ryde (IoW) and Brighton/Hove/Worthing, the Southern reopening Bungalow Town Halt (adjacent to Shoreham Airport). This afforded frequent electric train services to the centre of the three towns, and the Halt nameboard was furnished with a 'Shoreham Airport' suffix.

The Southern also sponsored a service to the Isle of Wight run jointly by Spartan Air Lines (a Pearson group subsidiary) and Railway Air Services. An important RAS service flew between London, Belfast and Glasgow, with a branch route to the Isle of Man, which was an all-the-year-round service, by contrast with the summer-only services on the other routes.

In 1935 a company backed by the GWR and the SR was formed to take a substantial interest in the Channel Isles services of Jersey and Guernsey Airways.

The railways' part in air transport has been criticised on two mutually exclusive grounds: the first, that they were seeking to create a transport monopoly, the second, that their commitment was inadequate to make a real impact. One cannot have it both ways!

In fact, the companies' policies seem to have been sensible: to get an established footing in the new mode of transport, but to limit the financial commitment until the market could be tested. All the services, or practically all, operated at a loss, as did practically all airlines at this period, and the railways were in no position to be generous with the money of their shareholders. The Committee of Inquiry into Civil Aviation (the Cadman Committee) in 1938 considered that 'the railway companies are making a useful contribution to civil air development . . . they have provided capital and experience in a proper and constructive manner'.

The railway involvement with catering goes back to the stage-coach era, when the association of inn-keeping with stage-coach proprietorship was very close. The railways replaced the coaching inns first by refreshment rooms and then by railway hotels. Whereas in most countries catering for railways is commonly performed by contract, in Britain the railways have often, though by no means always, preferred to undertake it themselves.

The Great Western had an unfortunate initial experience at Swindon, where the company foolishly entered into a long-term contract with a caterer (whose undrinkable coffee was castigated by Brunel) in which a clause obliged them to stop every express train at Swindon for ten minutes for refreshment purposes. The GWR eventually in 1895 had to buy out the contractor for £100,000. The experience was a searing one, which Paddington never forgot. Nevertheless, it did not initially persuade the railway to abandon letting refreshment rooms to contractors. But by the end of the century the GWR was running its own hotels which included not merely the Great Western Royal at Paddington but a luxurious resort hotel, the Tregenna Castle at St Ives. It also managed its refreshment rooms, as well as restaurant cars which were beginning to appear on express trains, and this continued until nationalisation.

The LMS and the LNER, from the date of grouping, managed their own hotels; their different policies have been discussed in Chapters 2 and 4. They also generally managed their own refreshment rooms with a few exceptions, mainly in Scotland. On the LMS, the Towle dynasty of celebrated hotel managers from the Midland Railway had established an enduring tradition of high-class business hotels in major cities and resort hotels at tourist centres. On the LNER hotel management was decentralised and came under the Divisional General Managers. Hotel managers on the LNER also had more responsibility and authority than their counterparts on the LMS.

The Southern had inherited a singularly complex variety of railway catering practices from its constituents. Perhaps surprisingly, the LSWR had never owned a London hotel. It did possess a couple of establishments, namely the quite imposing South Western Hotel at Southampton and the small Junction Hotel at Eastleigh, which it let out to contractors for many years. Refreshment rooms and restaurant cars on what became the Southern's South Western Division continued to be run by Spiers & Pond for some years after grouping, although the contract then passed to Frederick Hotels.

The LBSC brought to the Southern a wide variety of practices. The Grosvenor Hotel at Victoria and the refreshment rooms at that station were run by Gordon Hotels, and this continued throughout the lifetime of the Southern Railway.

166

Other contractors, Bertrams, managed the London and Paris Hotel at Newhaven and the remaining Brighton line refreshment rooms; but the Pullman Car Company provided train catering both in its own cars and in the pantry cars later built by the Southern for certain electric train sets.

The South Eastern section was peculiar in that the railway directly managed the Charing Cross Hotel and the nearby Craven Hotel, as well as the Cannon Street Hotel (until it was converted by the Southern Railway to an office block). But other hotels such as the Lord Warden at Dover and the Imperial at Hythe were run by contractors. There was also variety in refreshment room catering. Memory recalls a meal provided by popular caterers in a refreshment room below the present Blackfriars Station with the cutlery stamped 'LC&DR'!

Looking over the lifetime of the companies, the hotel business was generally profitable, though a few hotels were unsatisfactory and were sold soon after nationalisation, notably the Felix Hotel at Felixstowe which had been a GER showpiece. The reputation of railway hotels stood high, though many of the buildings were old-fashioned and unduly expensive to maintain and to heat in the winter.

Restaurant car services were generally popular and were, where necessary, subsidised as constituting an essential element in promoting rail travel. It was the refreshment rooms that incurred most criticism and fathered the legend of the railway sandwich that featured in many music-hall jokes. These rooms were undoubtedly the Cinderella of the Hotels Departments; perhaps more energetic management, not treated as the poor relation of the much more glamorous work of hotel-keeping, could have made many improvements.

Considering the conglomerate character of the four companies, two very different views have been expressed. One is, that so wide a range of activities distracted the boards and the General Managers from their main task of running the railways as efficiently as possible. This view certainly influenced the civil servants and politicians who decided that under nationalisation the docks, the road transport interests and the catering services should be taken away and put under separate managerial control.

The other view is that the companies should have anticipated the long-term decline in the railways' share of the nation's transport and should have diversified even more energetically than they did, closing down large sections of the rail network and replacing them with railway-owned road services.

Perhaps, with two such diametrically opposed views as to what the railways should have done, the middle course that was actually steered by the boards and managements had a good deal of justification.

CHAPTER 13

Partners or Rivals?

Throughout the nineteenth century, successive British Governments were unable to form any consistent policy towards railways. In the early railway age, political figures as different as the Duke of Wellington, James Morrison, MP, and W.E. Gladstone were inclined to regard railways as public utilities which should be planned as well as regulated by the State. Parliament at times seemed willing to undertake what nowadays would be termed a planning role, as when in 1836 the Speaker of the House of Commons, presumably reflecting the view of the House, announced that the proposed South Eastern and London & Brighton railways would have to share tracks as far as Redhill, because, in his words, 'no second outlet for a railway would be allowed to the South'.

But this restrictive view soon lapsed. It was after all the age of *laissez-faire* in business, of free trade and free competition. Parliament was at times swamped with railway Bills which it did not feel able to reject. Some led to the construction of competing systems, but others authorised railway amalgamations leading to the creation of large and sometimes monopolistic concerns. Occasionally Parliament rebelled against the pressures and threw out a proposed amalgamation as being against the public interest. But this vacillation, this lack of any consistent policy towards railway construction and ownership, continued right up to the grouping. The group companies represented neither clear territorial systems as in France, nor keenly competing routes over all major traffic flows, as in the USA. A glance at the Railway Clearing House map of the railways between 1923 and 1948 makes this obvious.

How far then did competition survive between the wars?

Competition can exist in charges or in quality of service. In charges it only persisted in the sense that both passengers and traders could enjoy a benefit from competitive fares and rates which were departures from the strict mileage principle where two or more railways offered services between the same points, the shortest distance determining the fares or rates to be charged by all the railways. Some of these were of course sensible – the Euston to Manchester (London Road) fare for a journey of 187 miles was applied to St Pancras–Manchester (Central), 190 miles, and Marylebone–Manchester (Central) 212 miles. Some were relics of a past age of unbridled competition, as when a competitive rate for goods sent by the Midland Railway's circuitous route from London to Bristol via Derby and Birmingham (258 miles) was the same as the GWR direct route of 118 miles. Railway enthusiasts with a taste for lengthy explorations of the rail network could enjoy surprising benefits from these competitive fares!

Broadly, however, with standard fares based on distance and standard freight rates similarly based, opportunities for competition in charging were limited. Of course, much of the freight traffic was carried at 'exceptional rates' below the standard, but the operation of the undue preference prohibition meant that the railways found it wise to work on the principle that 'dog does not eat dog', and to refrain from quoting an exceptional rate that could embarrass another railway. This process could easily work in reverse, so that consultation through the medium of the appropriate committee of the Railway Clearing House was generally undertaken before any major change in charges was given effect.

If price competition scarcely existed, there was considerable competition in prestige and public relations. The rather absurd rush to proclaim ownership of 'the most powerful passenger locomotive' has already been mentioned. In other ways, such as the publicity given to locomotive performance in the exchange trials of 1925 between the GWR and the LNER, rivalry existed.

170

But if one tries to measure the benefits to the customer from this competitive spirit, they are not very obvious. The rather slow progress towards faster travel and reductions in journey time up to 1937 has already been mentioned. The 8¼ hour London–Edinburgh timing agreed after the end of the 1888 racing between the East and West Coast Companies continued to inhibit competition on this route, as did the two-hour agreement between the LMS and the GWR for the London–Birmingham traffic, for far too long.

Competition in theory continued, for instance between the LMS and the LNER in the service from London to Leeds and Bradford, but one cannot say that it led to a higher quality of service than existed on the monopoly routes such as London–Liverpool (LMS) or London–Newcastle (LNER). The GWR served Bristol (monopolised) quite as well as it did Exeter (competitive with the SR).

The companies decided in the depression years that economies could be obtained from eliminating the remaining elements of competition between themselves. In 1932 three 'pools' were established, one between the LMS and the LNER, one between the LMS, LNER and GWR, and one between the LMS and the GWR. The pools covered all competitive passenger fare receipts, as well as freight traffic. An LMS, LNER, GWR and SR pool to cover all parcels traffic followed, and came into operation at the beginning of 1934. There was also a pool of passenger receipts from points west of Exeter between the GWR and the Southern.

The basis was the actual receipts between the competitive points over the years 1928, 1929 and 1930, which established percentage shares for each company. During the period of the agreements, all the receipts, less a fixed percentage allowance for working expenses, were paid into the pool and then divided in the agreed proportions.

The object was to reduce competitive canvassing for traffic which sometimes resulted in freight travelling by the longer rather than the shorter route, involving greater cost of carriage but no greater corresponding receipts. In this the pooling achieved some success, though it has been said that a certain amount of competitive canvassing continued *sub rosa* because it was advantageous to retain the deduction for working expenses. A net receipts pool instead of a gross receipts one would of course have eliminated this incentive.

In 1933, following the creation of the London Passenger Transport Board, and of a Standing Joint Committee of the main line railways and the Board, a pool of receipts from main line railway and London Transport fares within the Board's statutory area was set up. Its main effect was to remove the sting of competition between the Southern Railway and the Underground, which had already been reduced by the understanding on 'spheres of influence' reached between Sir Herbert Walker and Lord Ashfield, Chairman of the Underground group and later of London Transport. The pool proportions were 62 per cent to the LPTB and 38 per cent (of which the Southern's share at 25½ per cent was much the greatest) to the main lines.

With these pooling arrangements, one may perhaps wonder at the apparent resurgence of competition in the later 1930s, when the two hour 'understanding' over journey time to Birmingham and the 8¼ hour agreement for the Edinburgh services were thrown to the winds. The challenge of Gresley's streamlined High Speed Trains was taken up eagerly by the LMS, and speed records, culminating in *Mallard*'s celebrated if momentary 126mph, were made in the spirit of a sporting contest. But this was in no sense commercial competition, only a prestige exercise, greatly enjoyed by the railway staff involved as well as by the public.

In every way the railways were drawing closer together as the years passed. The regular meetings in the Railway Clearing House conferences and committees, between officers, and in the Railway Companies Association between the Chairmen, formed a basis for reaching agreements over a wide range of subjects in which the railways' interests were common. The pressure of financial stringency also drew the railways together. Wasting their substance in competition, except for a few publicity exploits, was not acceptable and what Kipling called 'ties of common funk' enforced co-operation. Agreement on common action over road powers and air powers was a good example, the former leading to the joint purchase of Carter Paterson and Pickfords, the latter to the joint formation of Railway Air Services. This process culminated in the 'Square Deal' campaign of 1938–9. Joint action and a single policy approach to most questions of course became automatic under war conditions when the general managers sat together almost daily in the Railway Executive Committee.

After the war the railways drew even closer together under the threat of nationalisation. The Railway Companies Association had set up a Post-war Planning Commission as long ago as 1942, and it produced reports covering a variety of ways in which the railways intended closer co-operation if they were left to run their own businesses. A net receipts pool between the LMS and LNER was under consideration for a time. There was agreement on the principle of an exchange of penetrating lines such as the LMS enclaves in South Wales. Joint lines also were to be eliminated; the LMS was particularly emphatic on the desirability of its absorbing the Cheshire Lines (which was profitable), in return for handing over to the LNER the Midland & Great Northern Joint (which was unprofitable)!

After the war a certain amount of publicity material began to be issued under the heading 'British Railways' – with the company initials following. It was a hint of things to come. Did the railways make nationalisation easier by having already come so much closer together than in earlier days? The answer is probably that, despite the competitive basis upon which railways had been built, and despite the lingering traces of competition in the groups as created by the 1921 Railways Act, competition between railways had become utterly irrelevant because of the threats from outside, especially from road transport. The railways had no option but to forget rivalry and to pool all their resources to fight the common enemy.

CHAPTER 14
'Home Rails'

Only the middle-aged or elderly can today remember when a major section of the daily lists of the Stock Exchanges bore the 'Home Rails' title. And the passage of time has allowed a common misconception to appear. Today, more than 30 years after nationalisation, many people are inclined to assume that the railways had to be taken over because they were bankrupt. This is quite incorrect. It would be equally untrue to suggest that the railways were nationalised because they made excessive profits through overcharging. The facts are that in the first half of the twentieth century the main line railways were earning quite substantial net receipts in total and this continued after nationalisation, well into the 1950s. Although the return on the companies' equity capital, ie the ordinary stocks, was always modest and sometimes non-existent, they generally managed (with a few lapses) to pay the full preference dividends and never failed to meet their debenture interest. So there was no question of bankruptcy.

Of course the day of the railway mania was long past, when fortunes could be made (and lost) by speculating in railway shares. By the end of the nineteenth century the principal railways' stocks were respectable investments; those of the four giants, the LNWR, GWR, MR and NER, in fact were regarded as gilt-edged. 'Midland Railway Consols' were the sort of security that a stockbroker would recommend to clients seeking security above all, the country clergymen and widows of small means.

The first world war marked the end of this era. As happened later in the second world war, the Government took over the railways, assuming responsibility for the expenditure and pocketing the receipts, while the shareholders were guaranteed the continuation (broadly) of their immediate pre-war dividends. In both wars the railways carried swollen traffics but this produced no benefits for the shareholders. In 1914–18, the Government decided that wages must be increased (which was fully justified) but refused to allow charges to be raised to compensate for the additional costs. In consequence, a railway wages bill of £47 millions in 1913 had been increased to £173 millions in 1921. In 1919 the Government had also conceded an eight-hour day. But not until 1920 was the Government willing to increase rates and charges. So the railways, which in 1913 had had net receipts of £45.6 millions, by 1921 were actually in deficit.

The railways began to recover their financial equilibrium once they were permitted to raise their charges, and soon afterwards the grouping took effect. Under the Railways Act 1921, the railways were allotted a 'standard revenue' (roughly the 1913 net revenue plus an allowance for capital raised subsequently), to obtain which their charges might be adjusted. But in no year was standard revenue earned; the actual earnings of the companies are summarised below and compared with 1913. The figures show the position in the first year after grouping (1923), six years later, when the economies from grouping should have taken effect (1929) and the worst after-effects of the general strike in 1926 should have worn off, in the worst year of the depression (1932), and with recovery well under way (1937):

	Railway Working Receipts		Companies' Net Revenues
	Gross	Net	
	£m.	£m.	£m.
1913	117	43	47
1923	196	39	46
1929	183	40	45
1932	145	26	29
1937	167	34	38

The decline in net earnings and profitability was of course reflected in dividends. The LMS paid an ordinary dividend of 7 per cent in 1924. Five years later, despite the savings from amalgamation, the dividend was no more than 4½ per cent in the last year which preceded the world depression. In several succeeding years the dividend was nil and the full dividends were not earned or paid on even the junior preference stocks. After the upturn in 1937, which was a good year for much of British industry, the ordinary dividend was only 1½ per cent.

The Great Western Railway had paid as much as 8 per cent in 1924. Even in the 'bad' years of the depression it was anxious, partly to preserve the marketability and the Stock Exchange price of its stocks, and partly for prestige reasons, to maintain the eligibility of its prior charges for investment by trustees. The requirement for this was a dividend maintained at not less than 3 per cent on the ordinary stock. Such a dividend was in fact always paid by the GWR, but only by drawing quite substantially upon 'free' reserves which the GWR had built up and regarded as available for dividend equalisation. In 1932 the transfer from general reserve was no less than £1.1 million, which caused some raised eyebrows in the City of London.

Both the LNER and the Southern had what were known as 'split' stocks. The ordinary capital was divided into two parts, preferred and deferred. The preferred ordinary was entitled to a fixed dividend, after which the balance, if any, was distributed to the deferred shareholders. Such an arrangement of course increased the 'gearing' of the stocks, in Stock Exchange phraseology, and made the deferred ordinary a more speculative investment, its market price reacting strongly to upward or downward trends in revenues available for distribution.

The LNER, with its dependence upon freight traffic and the fortunes of heavy industry, saw its net revenues fall from £14 million in 1923 to £4.6 million in the strike year, 1926, recovering to £12.2 million in 1927 but then falling to £7.2

million in 1932, recovering to £10.1 million in 1937, with yet another setback to £6.7 million in 1938. These violent ups and downs, coupled with the 'gearing' of the equity stock, meant that while in the early years the preferred ordinary dividend of 5 per cent was paid and the deferred received 2½ per cent, in 1925 the latter stock received only 1 per cent and nothing at all thereafter. The preferred stockholders received only ¼ per cent in 1928, 3 per cent in 1929, ¼ per cent in 1930 and nothing from 1931 to 1933. In the worst of the depression even some prior charges – first and second preference stocks – did not receive their full dividends.

The Southern, despite escaping the worst effects of the industrial depression, found itself vulnerable to reduced public spending power as well as to road competition affecting its passenger traffic. Its net revenues, which had been £6.5 million in 1923, fell to £5.5 million in 1933, and only recovered to £6.2 million in 1937. So, in the worst years, Southern deferred ordinary stock, like that of the LNER, received no dividend and even the preferred ordinary did not receive the full amount.

The amalgamations had been expected to put the railways as a whole in an improved financial position, for two reasons. First of all, rationalisation or what economists like to call the economies of scale should have reduced expenditure. Secondly, a financially weaker company such as the Great Central would benefit from association with the much stronger North Eastern Railway. Both expectations were disappointed. The economies of scale were slower to appear and less substantial than had been hoped, and the long-standing depression in the heavy industries weakened those parts of the groups that had previously been most profitable – those serving the North East, or the South Wales coal mining areas, for instance.

The railways could do nothing about the decline in coal, iron and steel or shipbuilding, but they could search for economies to offset the losses in receipts. Their activity in this field varied a great deal. Economies of scale were scarcely realis-

able on the GWR, which changed so little after 1923, and the
LNER's deliberate preference for decentralised management
also made rapid or arbitrary changes to secure economies
more difficult than on the strongly centralised LMS. Even so,
when revenues were hit by the depression in 1930 special
economy measures were taken by the LNER which in that
and the following year together produced savings of £4.25
millions, additional to those from the long-term reductions in
staff numbers and in the locomotive stock resulting from the
fall in traffic.

The Southern Railway was in a somewhat special position.
Its main concern was with improving its services through
electrification, which brought with it both increased traffic
and operating economies.

It was the LMS which was able, through its strongly centralised management, to pursue economies with an energy
that bordered on the ruthless. Mention has already been
made of the reorganisation of workshop practice to bring
down the repair costs of locomotives and rolling stock. To this
must be added the drive to secure better utilisation of motive
power through cyclical diagramming.

The LMS also achieved worthwhile savings in administra-
tive costs. When visiting the United States in 1927/8 the President of the Executive, Sir Josiah Stamp, was impressed by a
business efficiency expert named J.E. Murphy. Stamp persuaded Murphy to accept, on a commission basis, a contract
with the LMS to overhaul the design and number of forms
and documents required for management purposes, and to
effect economies in paper and printing costs. Murphy set up
the LMS 'Executive Research Office' (ERO) which did in
fact save a considerable amount of money, though of course
the appearance and quality of LMS paper were downgraded
considerably. The many forms bearing ERO reference
numbers survived on the London Midland Region well into
nationalisation.

With hindsight, one can argue that economies could have

been sought more effectively by discarding uneconomic sections of the railway, and by increasing labour productivity. To this there are two answers. First, the science (or art) of traffic costing had not yet grown up as it did after nationalisation and there was a general philosophy that to cover the heavy burden of fixed costs, traffic needed to be maximised, which involved taking the rough with the smooth, the branches along with the main lines. Secondly, becoming less labour-intensive means becoming more capital-intensive, and investment resources were always inadequate throughout the life of the companies. Lastly, road competition had not yet assumed the proportions that it did in the vast expansion of motor traffic after the second world war.

Looking at the other side of the account, could the railways have done more to increase their receipts so as to earn the standard revenue to which the Government had said they were entitled? The door was open to them to manipulate their charges, the standard rates, upwards or downwards, subject to the approval of the Railway Rates Tribunal. With the exception of two small percentage increases, of 7 per cent in 1927 and a further 5 per cent in 1937, the railways felt that raising rates would be counter-productive. Equally, reductions to attract more traffic had many pitfalls because of the undue preference clauses, but selective quotation of exceptional rates and agreed charges was done wherever commercially justified.

Despite the difficulties on the revenue side, and the rather poor dividend records, it would scarcely be accurate to describe the companies as poverty-stricken. They had large reserves in liquid form – cash and quickly realisable securities – amounting to £71 millions even at the end of the disastrous strike year of 1926.

The fact that the railways earned, in total, substantial net revenues yet were unable to pay what might be regarded as a commercial rate of return on their equity stocks, is bound to raise a query as to whether their book capital was excessive, and whether an ordinary business would have written down its capital liabilities to a more realistic figure in relation to its future profit expectations. There is no simple answer to this question because the statutory form of railways accounts – the so-called double account system – did not show capital receipts as liabilities and capital expenditure as assets, only the balance between capital receipts and expenditure being shown in the balance sheet as an asset according to whether the expenditure exceeded the receipts, or vice versa. This figure therefore was an historical record, not a valuation of assets. There was no possibility of writing up or writing down the railway capital except by obtaining an Act of Parliament.

An important result of the unsatisfactory dividend position was inability to raise new capital through the orthodox means of a Stock Exchange issue. How then did they finance their investment needs?

First, a large part of the requirements were met from internal sources, the renewal funds built up from revenue. In addition the railway superannuation fund balances were deposited with the companies and were a source of finance, although of course interest was payable on the deposits.

Secondly, Government assistance became available in several ways The Development (Loan Guarantees and Grants) Act 1929 enabled the railways to carry out some capital improvements on the basis of the Government making grants for a maximum period of 15 years to cover the interest charges on the approved works. In addition the Government abolished the tax, going back to stage-coach days, known as Railway Passenger Duty. It had first been imposed in 1832, and in 1842 was established as a charge of 5 per cent upon the gross receipts from passengers, except that after 1844 the Parliamentary trains for third-class passengers were exempt. It was in effect a sort of luxury tax on travel in first or second class and became an anachronism that eventually was abolished in 1929 on condition that the railways would capitalise the amount paid in tax at 5 per cent, and then spend 90 per cent of this notional amount of capital on approved new works.

The object was to stimulate the economy and relieve unemployment. The companies put forward various schemes, in total rather more than the notional sum representing the capitalised value of the saving in tax liability. The GWR carried out works at freight depots and brought forward the locomotive building programme. The LMS had similar projects; the LNER among other new works provided for track widening on the Great Eastern section; the Southern went in for passenger rolling stock and more electrification.

Then in 1933, through the medium of the Government-backed Railway Finance Corporation and the London Electric Transport Finance Corporation, capital at 2½ per cent and 2¾ per cent was made available to the railways and London Transport for approved schemes designed to relieve unemployment and assist economic recovery. The works undertaken on this basis have been described in Chapter 8.

The arrangements under which the Government took over control of the railways in the second world war will be described in Chapter 15. From the point of view of the railway investor the main effect was that a fixed rental was paid for the greater part of the war by the Government to the companies, which was considerably less than the monies that the railways would have retained in the same period had they been left under private control.

The 1941 Railway Control Agreement provided for the following annual rental payments, which it is interesting to compare with the standard revenues to which, under the 1921 Railways Act, the Government had said the railways were entitled:

	1941 Control Agreement	Standard Revenue 1921 Act
	£m.	£m.
LMS	14.75	20.6
LNER	10.14	15.2
GWR	6.67	8.5
SR	6.61	7.1

The above rental payments, added to £4.83m for the LPTB, amounted to £43 million in total. Robert Bell in his *History of the British Railways during the War 1939–45* points out that these fixed amounts represented only 67 per cent of the actual net revenues of the companies in 1941, under 48 per cent in 1942, 41 per cent in 1943 and 48 per cent in 1944. In other words, the 'controlled undertakings' received in these four years only £174 million for the intensive use of their property and services out of a total actually earned of £350 million.

Had the railways been allowed to retain their hard-earned wartime net revenues, both to provide for post-war rehabilitation of overworked assets and to pay dividends that in some measure would reflect both increased traffic and the effects of inflation, they would have been in a strong position at the end of the war. When they were nationalised, however, the basis upon which railway stocks were compulsorily acquired reflected only the Stock Exchange valuation of the revenue prospects under Government control.

A new British Transport 3 per cent stock was created and the following amounts were allocated in exchange for the railway equity stocks.

£100 LMS	Ordinary	= £29.50 British Transport 3%
£100 LNER	Preferred Ordinary	= £ 7.31 British Transport 3%
£100 LNER	Deferred Ordinary	= £ 3.62 British Transport 3%
£100 GWR	Ordinary	= £59.06 British Transport 3%
£100 SR	Preferred Ordinary	= £77.62 British Transport 3%
£100 SR	Deferred Ordinary	= £24.00 British Transport 3%

The valuation of the railway stocks was based upon the average of the Stock Exchange quotations, either for the period February–June 1945 (before the general election) or 1–8 November 1946 (before publication of the Transport Bill) whichever was the more favourable.

Sir Ronald Matthews of the LNER protested that the terms of this enforced take-over 'would bring a blush of shame to the leathery cheek of a Barbary pirate'. The Chancellor of the Exchequer, Dr Hugh Dalton, took an opposite view. In the House of Commons he argued that the Government was probably being too generous. In a famous (or infamous) reference to 'a very poor bag of assets' he went on to add: 'The permanent way is badly worn. The rolling stock is in a state of great dilapidation. The railways are a disgrace to the country.' Neither statement need be taken at its face value; Sir Ronald, however, had the keener sense of humour.

The massive exchange of securities, involving about 1,250,000 separate holdings, was carried out by the Registration Offices of the four railways, progressively transferring the accounts to the Bank of England as the Registrar of British Transport Stock. So there disappeared from Britain's Stock Exchanges the markets in 'Home Rails' which had been so important and active for well over a century.

CHAPTER 15

The Railways at War

The British nation, which between the wars had been quietly changing to increased reliance upon road transport, suddenly discovered in 1939 that the railways would be essential not only for victory but even for survival. Oil fuel, carried from overseas at heavy cost in sunken ships and lost lives, not to mention scarce foreign exchange, was needed on a huge scale for the fighting services; all other users had to be severely rationed. The railways, still consuming almost exclusively home-produced fuel, had to replace long-distance road transport. In addition, of course, they had to carry the huge extra volume of wartime Government traffic. Luckily, the railways' inherent capacity for bulk movement, that had been so under-utilised in peacetime, could now be exploited to the full.

Planning for the wartime role of the railways had begun in 1937 when the Ministry of Transport held preliminary discussions with the general managers; when the Munich crisis of 1938 arose, the Government quickly appointed a Railway Executive Committee consisting of the four main line general managers and the Vice-Chairman of the London Passenger Transport Board, though only as an advisory body for the time being.

An REC had previously been constituted in 1914 when, under the rather incongruously named Regulation of the Forces Act 1871, the Government had assumed control of the railways for the duration of the emergency. In 1938–9 the second REC became the intermediary between the Minister of Transport and the company managements.

The REC's functions were never defined with precision but rather evolved. It was certainly not just a post office for Government directives; the traffic was two-way and the REC frequently made recommendations to the Minister for Government action. The REC had no less than 16 committees dealing with all aspects of railway work under the emergency conditions.

The need for the REC to continue meeting under possible air attack led the railways to accept an offer from the LPTB to adapt a disused tube station, Down Street on the Piccadilly Line, as a bomb-proof office. Entrance from street level was through an inconspicuous door; during air raids or other cases of need, access was by travelling in the driving cab of a tube train that would make, if authorised, a special stop at a short length of platform left accessible for this purpose. For a brief period this shelter was borrowed by the War Cabinet pending completion of its own deep-level centre.

The preparatory planning of the railways included evacuation centres for both management and train control offices, outside London. The Southern's wartime headquarters was at Deepdene House, near Dorking, and the Great Western's at Aldermaston, near Reading, where several houses were occupied. The LMS took over The Grove, near Watford, where many temporary buildings were erected in the grounds to supplement the accommodation in the main mansion. The LNER scattered its departments: 'HQ1', a country house near Whitwell in Hertfordshire named The Hoo, housed the Chief General Manager and the Divisional General Manager, Southern Area. Other departments were dispersed over the outer suburban districts.

Control offices similarly were moved to safer areas – the Southern's South Western Division to Woking; the LNER Southern Area's Western Section to Gerrard's Cross and the Eastern to Shenfield, for example.

The wisdom of these moves was shown when in the London bombing there was major destruction at Waterloo and London Bridge on the Southern, at King's Cross on the LNER, at Paddington on the GWR, and at numerous other railway stations and offices.

The most obvious result of the creation of the REC was the operation of the railways, for war purposes, as a unified system; the preliminary planning, carried out by the Operating Committee, had covered the early evacuation of civilians from London, since the City was expected to be an immediate target of enemy bombing, the mass movement of men called up, and the despatch of two British Expeditionary Forces, one for France and one for the Mediterranean, and other overseas garrisons.

In September 1939 the balloons went up – literally – and the earlier planning work was translated into action with remarkable smoothness. On 31 August 1939 the REC took control of the railways as the agent of the Minister of Transport, with Sir Ralph Wedgwood (who had retired in March of that year from the LNER Chief General Managership) as its Chairman. With the co-operation of London Transport, the evacuation from London was carried out for children and certain classes of adult such as the sick or aged. Congestion at the main London termini was avoided by despatching the evacuees by London Transport services to such suburban stations as Ealing Broadway on the GWR, Bowes Park on the LNER, Watford on the LMS and Wimbledon on the Southern, where main line trains were joined. Over 600,000 persons in total were carried to the reception areas from London and over 700,000 from other evacuation zones such as Liverpool, Tyneside and Glasgow.

But civilian evacuation was not to be a once-for-all operation. In May 1940, with the advent of air raids, more programmes of evacuation specials had to be arranged; in 1944 the flying bomb attacks caused another mass movement by rail away from London and South East England.

In accordance with pre-arranged plans, the initial movement of troops to the theatres of war was concentrated upon two ports, Glasgow and Southampton. The first British Expeditionary Force consisted of reinforcements for overseas garrisons, and was quickly conveyed to the port of Glasgow

187

over three days in 22 special trains. The second and larger Force required the provision of 261 special trains routed to Southampton, for France.

These carefully planned civilian and military movements were in strong contrast to the methods of rapid improvisation with which the railways had to complement the rescue by the 'little ships' of the British and Allied troops stranded at Dunkirk. The whole operation had to be arranged at very short notice with no previous information about numbers, locations or timing. 'Operation Dynamo', as it was coded, involved the transport of over 330,000 men from South Coast ports to a wide range of inland destinations. The four railways through the REC Operating Committee rapidly formed a pool of 186 trains which completed 620 journeys. The Southern Railway handled this huge traffic, arriving in unpredictable numbers at unpredictable ports, with improvised local controls and sub-controls, despatching the troop and ambulance trains to camps all over Britain, for the critical eight days between 27 May and 4 June 1940, from ports as widely separated as Dover and Southampton.

By contrast, a carefully planned operation was the rail component in 'Overlord' under which over 80 special trains were run daily between 3 June and 20 June 1944 to move troops and supplies into the forward areas for the invasion of Europe. This movement of course continued after D-Day, nearly 4,800 specials being run for the Forces between D-Day and VE-Day.

The combined traffics – those for Government purposes and the normal train service for civilians – operated under several handicaps. Perhaps the most severe was the blackout. This involved both the hooding and the reduction in light intensity of colour-light signals, the drastic reduction in station lighting and especially marshalling yard lighting. Locomotive cabs had to be sheeted to exclude the fiery glow from the firebox door. Blue lamps in passenger carriages were installed and later replaced by box-like shades which cast a small beam downwards from slits and made it just possible to read. In 1940, when the threat of invasion appeared, station and signalbox names were removed and this anonymity, especially in the blackout, created many problems for passengers unfamiliar with the area.

Some half a million special trains were run during the six years of war over and above the regular timetabled service, fairly equally divided between passenger and freight specials. Many new flows of traffic emerged and these involved unfamiliar routeing arrangements. In October 1941 the four railways issued their staffs with new route-books, designed to avoid the congestion of key points and based on the principle that the railways were to be operated as a unified system without regard to company boundaries.

Freight traffic was speeded up by several devices. All private owners' wagons were requisitioned by the Minister and put into common user. The relaxation of wagon examination requirements at exchange points helped, as did the discontinuance of individual number-taking at such points and its replacement by bulk number-taking to enable the wagon availability position to be monitored.

To ensure that wagons did not travel with inadequate loads, and to reduce wasted mileage, a system of 'nominated loading' was introduced under which consignments were accepted only on specific days for through loading to destination. Economies were also achieved by the institution of 'convoy trains' (which nowadays would be termed block trains). These avoided marshalling yards and ran through to destination. Many conveyed coal to London and the South of England from the major mining areas, particularly the North-East Coast where the railway had to replace coastal shipping services which before the war had brought enormous quantities of coal down the eastern seaboard to the Thames and other ports.

The new traffic movements overloaded the existing cross-London railway routes. These were in any case extremely vulnerable to bomb damage. Accordingly, new north–south connections in an outer ring around London were provided at Reading (GWR/SR), Oxford (GWR/LMS), Calvert (LMS/LNER), Bletchley (LMS), Sandy (LMS/LNER), Bowes Park (LNER), Gospel Oak (LMS), Romford (LMS/LNER), and Staines (GWR/SR). Other major new operating facilities included four-tracking between Gloucester and Cheltenham, and widenings between York and Northallerton, as well as new and extended marshalling yards at various places.

New building of locomotives was drastically reduced during the war to free railway workshops for war production. However, it was decided in December 1941 that the standard LMS 2–8–0 freight locomotive should be built in substantial numbers and a good proportion was sent to Persia (Iran) to provide extra motive power for the rail supply route to Soviet Russia.

Soon afterwards the Ministry commissioned from the North British Locomotive Company, which had the assistance of the LMS Chief Draughtsman, a design for a wartime Austerity 2–8–0 locomotive intended for eventual service overseas. It embodied maximum economy in the use of scarce materials as well as simplicity in maintenance. These locomotives were built in quantity and until required for shipment overseas were lent to the home railways where they were· of considerable assistance for the time being. Some 450 were thus loaned, and another 500 were run in by the railways before despatch overseas.

Despite the oil shortage, the LMS and LNER built 50 diesel-electric shunters, which were particularly suitable and economic for work at military depots and camps, a number being sent overseas.

Some assistance was obtained from the temporary use of American 2–8–0 locomotives designed to work on European railways after the invasion. Some 400 of these were available between arrival in this country and their despatch to the newly liberated territories.

All these new locomotives were intended to be used exclusively for freight purposes. The Ministry had in fact instructed the REC that only freight or mixed-traffic locomotives might be built for the duration of the war. The way in which Bulleid's batch of Merchant Navy 4–6–2s in 1942 met this qualification is a mystery!

Wagon construction was still needed to handle swollen wartime traffics and special purpose wagons for tank transport, for instance, had to be provided. In the middle of the war, a standard all-steel mineral wagon of 16 tons capacity – known as the MWT wagon – was designed and built in very large numbers.

New passenger carriage construction came to a halt, but special work such as the conversion of stock into ambulance trains and provision of special vehicles for the use of the Prime Minister, the Supreme Allied Commander, and the Commander-in-Chief, Home Forces, was undertaken.

Passenger services had to be carried on despite difficulties. The Government decided, after studying the possibilities, that rationing of travel by the issue of permits was not practicable, apart from sleeping car reservations. Instead, voluntary rationing was urged by a propaganda campaign, largely based on the famous slogan 'Is Your Journey Really Necessary?' Of course, the overcrowding and delays imposed by wartime conditions automatically discouraged much travel, but people still wanted – and needed – holidays, and pressure on the railways at the usual holiday periods was intense. There was a certain reluctance, on general policy grounds, on the part of the Ministry of War Transport to authorise the REC to run relief trains for holiday crowds even when stock and locomotives happened to be available.

Better utilisation of passenger accommodation was obtained by the abolition of first class seating in the London suburban area from October 1941 and the permanent raising of intermediate seat rests to permit four-a-side seating in all main line third class compartments.

The civilian or normal passenger train service was drastically reduced at the outbreak of war but gradually restored, until early in 1940 about 75 per cent of the pre-war mileage was being run. Restaurant car services withdrawn in September 1939 were also restored on a restricted basis until they were again reduced in 1942 and completely withdrawn in April 1944 to help to release every possible resource for the D-Day preparations. After the successful landings and the opening up of the Western Front, train services were again improved in October 1944.

Speeds of course were reduced; an overall line speed limit of 60mph was imposed for the duration. After experience of the handicap imposed by the original drastic reduction in speeds to 25mph whenever an air raid warning was in force, from February 1941 trains ran normally by day during warning periods; by night, trains were stopped, cautioned and allowed to proceed at a maximum speed of 30mph.

While the railways of Great Britain escaped the wholesale destruction of many railway systems on the Continent – in Germany, France, Italy and Holland especially – damage by enemy bombing was widespread and continued over a long period. In all, there were over 9,000 incidents involving delay or damage to the railways during the 5½ years of the war in Europe. After the intensive conventional bombing had diminished, the flying bomb attacks in 1944/5 affected the railways in London and the South East quite severely, with 1,400 incidents and 102 direct hits on railway installations.

Rail services also tended to be disrupted by UXB incidents – actual or suspected unexploded bombs in the vicinity. If, for instance, an unexploded parachute mine was located within a quarter of a mile of the track, the train service had to be suspended until the mine had been rendered harmless.

It is impossible, even in summary, to chronicle the other wartime activities of the four great companies – the exploits, and the tragedies, for example, of the railway steamers requisitioned by the Admiralty. Some were used as transports and crossed the Atlantic on convoy duties; others were converted to hospital carriers. Many took part in the Dunkirk evacuation and actions in other parts of the world; many were sunk. The conversion of railway workshops to war purposes is a long story of which only one or two sample extracts can be given here. Crewe and Horwich works of the LMS, for instance, turned out no fewer than 642 tanks for the Army. Swindon produced bombs and aircraft wings; Derby undertook major repairs to bomber aircraft. All the railway shops produced many components, for tanks and aircraft and also pre-fabricated bridges.

The work of the railwaymen – and railway women, of whom there were no less than 60,000 by 1944, carrying out former men's jobs – has been told quite picturesquely in several books sponsored by the companies soon after the end of the war. The railways released a very large number of staff to the forces of whom over 3,500 lost their lives. A considerable number of senior railway officers were assigned to important Government posts, either military or civilian.

The financial arrangements under which the railways were operated on Government account during the war were defined in two Railway Control Agreements. The first, in February 1940, guaranteed the railways as a 'floor' the average of their net revenues for 1935, 1936 and 1937. If the net earnings exceeded these amounts, the excess would be divided between the railways and the Exchequer on a 50/50 basis until the railways received their standard revenue under the 1921 Railways Act. Any excess over this ceiling would be paid to the Exchequer.

In September 1941 the Government insisted upon changing to a fixed rental, as already described on page 182, instead of sharing the net receipts. Although the amount of the rental was slightly higher than the floor of the 1940 Agreement, it was substantially lower than the ceiling, and in practice, having regard to the net receipts the railways actually earned, was much less favourable to the companies, although arrangements were incorporated providing for eventual payments to the companies after the war for arrears of maintenance and abnormal wear and tear – which were never implemented because of nationalisation.

At the end of the war, instead of cash compensation, the railways received (and greatly appreciated) a special message of thanks from Mr Winston Churchill and another from General Eisenhower, the Supreme Allied Commander. Yet only a couple of years later a Chancellor of the Exchequer could utter his famous 'very poor bag of assets' sneer. So short are memories – and the gratitude of politicians!

CHAPTER 16

Death of the Companies

In the middle of the war, when one might have expected the problems and tasks of the immediate future to be so demanding as to exclude long-range planning, two things happened. In 1942 the railway chairmen, meeting in the Railway Companies Association, decided to start thinking about the post-war role of the railways. The Association set up a committee for this purpose chaired by Sir Eric Gore-Browne, then Deputy Chairman of the Southern. Almost at the same time in the Ministry of War Transport the Director General, Sir Cyril Hurcomb, circulated a paper to his colleagues on the same subject. But the underlying approach and ideas were very different in Palace Chambers, the office of the RCA, and in Berkeley Square House, the labyrinthine home of the MWT.

The chairmen looked forward to a return to private control, as well as private ownership, of the railways, following the winding-up of the Railway Control Agreement. They had rejected a rather bold proposal from the Gore-Browne Committee for the virtual unification of the railways by a financial merger. Instead, they envisaged a continuation of the closer co-operation between the groups that had appeared under the pressures of war. Road competition would be met both by extending the existing railway investments in road haulage and by implementing the agreements provisionally reached with the Road Haulage Association at the end of the Square Deal campaign in 1939. Many ideas for improving the quality of railway service were to be tried out as soon as peace returned, and it was also decided, where conditions allowed, to draw upon the experience of the American railroads.

But in Berkeley Square House it was being agreed between

the senior civil servants that a return to pre-war organisation, and allowing the railways to deal with future road competition on the basis of the Square Deal principles – even though these had been accepted by the Government in 1939 – would not be satisfactory. Sir Cyril Hurcomb suggested that some form of what he called a public control board would be needed. Colleagues went further and minuted that the railways were 'ripe for nationalisation'. This proposition was going rather far for a Minister who was not a socialist, even though Lord Leathers was considered by the Chairmen to be unsympathetic to the railways. But he supported Sir Cyril Hurcomb sufficiently to tell the chairmen that he did not favour implementation of the Square Deal charter for railway freedom once the war ended, and that some more radical solution must be found. He made this clear in a speech in the House of Lords in 1943.

The civil servants accordingly, while stopping short of preparing a full-scale blueprint for railway nationalisation, played around (the word is not intended to be offensive) with possible forms of organisation incorporating a public control board. These led to the idea of subsidiary organisations below the top-level planning authority, one for each form of transport; in other words, there was to be a functional system of control rather than a geographical or regional one. An argument that seemed to weigh very strongly against the latter was the fact that under it the four railway companies would be the natural framework for the regional transport structures and would tend to dominate them. That was anathema in Berkeley Square House.

At this point one may ask whether the relations between the railways and the Ministry had been sweetened or soured by the close wartime contacts. The answer must be equivocal. At the top level, Sir Cyril Hurcomb and Sir William Wood had long enjoyed an excellent personal relationship – Wood having served in the Ministry with Hurcomb during and after the first world war. Sir James Milne's abilities were also greatly respected, as was shown later by the offer to him of the chairmanship of the future Railway Executive.

Relations with Sir Eustace Missenden of the Southern and Sir Charles Newton of the LNER were not on the same plane. At lower levels the 'meeting of minds' between railwaymen and civil servants was now and again soured by failure to appreciate each other's approach to a problem. Despite the wholehearted way in which the railways responded to all policy directives on important issues, there was an undercurrent of resentment from time to time among professional railwaymen at receiving instructions from those whom they considered amateurs. And civil servants sometimes felt that they were being faced with demands from the REC without the kind of supporting evidence that their training had led them to expect.

Accordingly, when the General Election of July 1945 returned a Labour Government to power with a very large majority, the new Minister of Transport (the word 'War' was soon dropped from his title), Alfred Barnes, found that his remit from the Party manifesto to nationalise transport had to some extent been anticipated by his civil servants. The next step was to develop the organisational proposals and to get them agreed by the Cabinet so that legislation could be drafted. The civil servants set to, under the guidance of Sir Cyril Hurcomb on major policy matters while an Assistant Secretary, Mr S.S. Wilson, was put in charge of the Bill's drafting. This task, despite the complexity of the measure – it ran to 136 pages, with 127 clauses and 13 schedules – was undertaken with the nearest thing to zest that a civil servant allows himself to display!

The Labour Party had been a long time evolving ideas about transport nationalisation. Railway nationalisation had been railway trade union policy since 1894, but the concept of integrated transport in the public sector had developed much later. The relative success of the London Passenger Transport Board in co-ordinating London railway, bus and tram services had led to a belief that the same recipe might be applied to transport on a nationwide scale. That intention was declared in the Labour Party's 1945 election manifesto 'Let Us Face the Future', but in view of the fact that Labour was not expected to win the election, it attracted less attention than it deserved from the railways.

During the period between the Labour Party's election victory on 5 July 1945 and the introduction of the Transport Bill on 28 November 1946, the railways had of course taken note of the Government's announcement on 19 November 1945 that it was the intention 'to bring transport services, essential to the economic well-being of the nation, under public ownership and control'. But on the one hand this very general statement gave little inkling of what was exactly in mind for the railways, and on the other, they were pre-occupied with many immediate problems among them shortages of coal, heavy arrears of maintenance and continuing pressure of traffic demands on a system strained by six years of war. The political proposals seemed pretty irrelevant when the severe winter of 1946–7 brought a fuel crisis and people shivered in icy rooms as electricity was cut off and gas pressures fell. That was also the period when the Ministry insisted that the railways should conserve coal by converting a number of locomotives to burn oil fuel. Government money was made available to meet the cost of the modifications to locomotive fireboxes and the fitting of tender fuel tanks, as well as for the fuelling installations on the ground at motive power depots. The railways regarded this as a panic measure but had no alternative but to put in schemes as directed.

The work had scarcely been completed when the coal crisis eased and, as the railways had anticipated, the disadvantages of burning oil in locomotives, in terms of pounds, shillings and pence, as well as the drain upon scarce foreign exchange, were seen to be unacceptable, and the policy was abruptly reversed. The oil fuel installations were removed and the taxpayer footed the bill for an ill-judged expedient.

These were real problems, which to many railwaymen seemed more important than whether or not shareholders and boards of directors were to continue to function. The planners inside the Ministry of Transport in fact seemed isolated from the world outside. There was virtually no contact between civil servants engaged in drafting the Bill and the railways, no consultation on organisation, and no drawing upon the experience of those in railway management. There had been a rather half-hearted invitation to the Railway Companies Association to make any comments they wished about future railway organisation, but there was no promise of any constructive discussions to follow such a submission. The RCA replied that the Chairmen would prefer to withhold comment until they saw what the Government had in mind.

So when the Bill was published its sweeping provisions, leading to the creation of a vast new British Transport Commission, created surprise. There was not merely shock and resistance to the idea of being nationalised, but widespread scepticism about the concept of a huge State public transport corporation in which the railways would be only one component. The Railway Companies Association decided to mount a campaign against the Bill and a team of General Managers' Assistants, of which the present author was one, was set up to co-ordinate and direct the propaganda.

The main effort was concentrated upon the production of posters carrying the message 'Stop the Transport Bill' and pamphlets publicising the good record of the railways under private ownership and arguing the anti-nationalisation case both in general and in detail. The LMS had already produced *A Record of Large-Scale Organisation and Management, 1923–1946* and the LNER followed with *Forward: The LNER Development Programme*. The Railway Companies Association now weighed in with 'Why Nationalise Transport?' in which the railway companies were joined by their old adversary the Road Haulage Association.

A general plea for the railways to be left alone was contained in a booklet entitled *British Railways and the Future*, which promised major improvements. Two polemical publications were *Criticisms of the Railways and the Replies* and a series of speakers' notes (for Conservative MPs) dealing with various proposals of the Transport Bill and the reasons for criticising them.

The LNER attempted to put forward a constructive suggestion in place of straight opposition. Sir Charles Newton persuaded his Board to sponsor what he termed the 'landlord and tenant' scheme. Under it, the Company would sell its track, structures, stations, etc, to the State and be granted a lease to operate train services on payment of a rental for use of the transferred assets. The purchase price would be used thoroughly to modernise the equipment, traction and rolling stock remaining with the Company.

This proposal was not altogether dissimilar to arrangements that had prevailed for a while in Italy and elsewhere in the past. It claimed to recognise the appropriateness of transport infrastructure being the property and concern of the State while retaining commercial enterprise for the actual management tasks. It was described in a pamphlet entitled *The State and the Railways: an Alternative to Nationalisation* which the present author was directed to draft. The scheme was launched at a press conference but received short shrift from the Minister.

It may be mentioned here that the railway lobby in Parliament – railway directors who were members of the Upper or the Lower House – had dwindled dramatically, while the number of railwaymen MPs had correspondingly increased. At the beginning of the century no less than 53 MPs had been railway directors; after July 1945 there were only two, compared with 30 railwaymen on the Government benches. So there was little chance of personal experience at board room level being drawn upon in a telling way during the debates.

The Bill was hustled through Parliament by the application

of the guillotine by the Government, so that no less than 37 clauses received no discussion in Committee and others had examination cut short. The complexity of the Bill is shown by the fact that no less than 421 Government amendments (many of course trifling) had to be inserted during its passage.

However, the actual portion relating to nationalisation of the railways was short. The relevant words were: 'the whole of the undertakings of the bodies of persons [specified in the Third Schedule to this Act] . . . shall, on the first day of January, nineteen hundred and forty-eight . . . vest by virtue of this Act in the Commission'. The Third Schedule listed 59 'railway undertakers' – a sinister phrase to describe the four main line railways, the London Passenger Transport Board and no less than 54 minor railways and joint lines.

On organisation, the Act merely provided that the British Transport Commission should be assisted by a public authority known as the Railway Executive in the discharge of its functions in regard to railways. The demise of the railway companies was thus inevitable; apparently no serious consideration was given to the alternative possibility of the Government simply acquiring their capital stocks which would have probably been the easiest method of nationalisation.

The Railway Executive was set up in shadow form immediately after the Bill passed into law. Each of the four main lines was to be represented at the highest level, and various officers were invited to assist in the preliminary planning before the take-over at midnight on 31 December 1947. The Government hastily gave permission for the former Great Central Hotel opposite Marylebone Station to be converted to office use by the Executive. The LNER had purchased it at the end of the war for a similar purpose but planning permission had previously been denied to the railway company.

Sir James Milne of the GWR was offered the chairmanship but declined it, whereupon it was offered to Sir Eustace Missenden of the Southern who accepted. A sort of musical chairs followed with the object of seeing that each company obtained a fair crack of the whip. The Commercial Member was David Blee, the GWR Goods Manager; the Operating and Marine Member V.M. (later Sir Michael) Barrington-Ward, Divisional General Manager, Southern Area, LNER, who had been a wartime Chairman of the REC Operating Committee. Civil Engineering went to J.C.L. (later Sir Landale) Train, Chief Engineer of the LNER; Mechanical and Electrical Engineering went to R.A. Riddles, a Vice-President and former Deputy CME of the LMS; and staff matters were put in charge of a trade unionist, W.P. Allen, General Secretary of the Associated Society of Locomotive Engineers and Firemen. Last, but very far indeed from least, the Deputy Chairmanship and the responsibility for public relations and stores were entrusted to a distinguished outsider, General Sir William (later Field-Marshal Lord) Slim of Burma fame.

Honour thus seemed to be satisfied, but in the Company headquarters offices soon to become Regional offices of British Railways, many preferred to sit tight and see what would happen after 1 January 1948. What actually happened of course is another story. The Company chairmen made their last speeches to the shareholders, declared their last dividends, and left the railway scene.

An ungrateful final General Meeting of shareholders of the LNER turned down a proposal to allot £63,000 to the Chairman and directors for loss of office, although passing an inexpensive resolution expressing appreciation of the services they had given the Company. By contrast, the officers clubbed together to produce an illustrated volume recording some highlights of the Company's history, and bearing their signatures attesting the long and happy relationship between the management and the Board. A copy was presented to each director.

Perhaps, however, more pain was felt at the death of the GWR than in any other case, since it had existed without a break from 1835, having itself been declared in the 1921 Act to comprise 'the amalgamated company', whereas the other three groups had only been born on 1 January 1922.

As a postscript, one may wonder what would have been the future of the railways had a Conservative Government come to power in 1945 and had nationalisation not taken place. Assuming an end to the Control Agreement, the financial arrangements would have led to substantial compensation to the companies for wartime arrears of maintenance at the prices current at the end of Government control. In addition a substantial claim for abnormal wear and tear was due to be met (also at current prices); war damage was also to be compensated and wartime works and rolling stock financed by the Government could have been taken over by the companies on favourable terms. So, if the railways had not been nationalised, the funds available to them would have been more than adequate for post-war rehabilitation, provided of course that the money could have been spent before it was eroded by inflation.

It is reasonable to assume that the companies would have diversified, especially by investing in road transport. If they had also been given the commercial freedom promised them by the Government in 1939, they could have staved off for a time the financial difficulties which first put British Railways in deficit in the mid-1950s. But the longer term outlook, had the railways still been privately owned when the post-war expansion of road transport got under way in the later 1950s and 1960s, would inevitably have been very difficult and some degree of Government assistance – and hence Government control of management – would scarcely have been escapable.

So, if we regret the passing of the GWR, the LMS, the LNER and the SR, we must accept that even if they had been reprieved in 1947, it seems unlikely that they could have survived into the 1970s without some drastic remodelling and some loss of identity. In fact, apart from the USA, whose recent railway history makes depressing reading, the four great railways of this country were almost the last survivors of large-scale private enterprise in rail transport. They had their shortcomings but also many achievements and they are remembered with affection by many who worked in them.

APPENDIX 1

The Scottish Experience

One may wonder, in retrospect, how far Scotland may have regretted the change of heart during the drafting of the Railways Act that led to the abandonment of the plan for a separate Scottish Railways Group. Did Scotland in fact benefit from its railways joining the English constituents of the LMS and the LNER? Was the assumed financial strength of the Southerners really needed to support the economy of the North?

Certainly after the 1914–18 war the Scottish railway companies faced difficulties. The fixing of railway wages and conditions of service on a national basis, following the establishment of a national negotiating machinery for the industry, was bound to raise their costs disproportionately to those of the English companies. The same effect was being experienced from the standardisation of the eight-hour day. And the Scottish lines had suffered, particularly the Highland and the North British, from overwork and undermaintenance during the war. The Highland, a lifeline of the Grand Fleet based on Scapa Flow, had been especially hard pressed and had only been able to cope with the aid of borrowed locomotives and the extensive use of other railways' rolling stock. The North British had a large claim against the Government for arrears of maintenance over which its doughty Chairman, William Whitelaw, fought a long and wearisome battle with the Government.

On the other hand the Scottish railways were by no means bankrupt. In 1922 the North British, though never very prosperous, still had net receipts of nearly £2½ millions and paid 1 per cent on its deferred ordinary stock after meeting its prior charges. The little 'Great North' paid 1½ per cent on its deferred ordinary. The future LMS constituents paid modest but respectable dividends in that year: the Caledonian 3½ per cent on its ordinary stock, the Glasgow & South Western 2½ per cent on the preferred ordinary and 1 per cent on the deferred ordinary and even the Highland paid 2 per cent on its ordinary stock.

The argument that the Scottish lines would enjoy financial support from their English partners looks, in retrospect, to have been rather illusory, if one considers the difficulty the LNER experienced from carrying the Great Central without the earnings

205

which the North Eastern was expected to bring into the group from the heavy industrial traffic of North East England. In fact, the Scottish Area was probably less of a drag on the LNER finances than the Great Central section of the Southern Area.

Moreover, the Caledonian had an excellent financial record as well as a soundly-built and, before the war, well-maintained railway. It can be argued that the long depression in the industrial belt of Central Scotland and on Clydeside was bound to hit both the Caledonian and the North British hard, as the LNER was to be hit by the slump in England's basic industries. But one may well feel that a single Scottish Railway Company, unifying all the systems, would have faced Scottish problems with Scottish business acumen, and that sensible solutions would have been found, for example the rationalisation of train services between Edinburgh and Glasgow, very much on the lines of what was eventually done by the Scottish Region of British Railways.

In fact, the success of the later BR Regional management in Scotland in unifying the railways without power struggles such as troubled the LMS are sufficient grounds for regretting that it could not have been done 25 years earlier.

Once the amalgamations were an accomplished fact, many in Scotland must have had second thoughts about them. All mergers tend, at any rate in the early stages, to lower staff morale and create anxieties and resentments. The new bosses are almost always more remote than the old ones and their actions often seem perverse or insensitive. Great skill is needed to handle these changes, especially where some element of national sentiment is involved.

On the LMS, the Scottish Division became almost identified with the Caledonian. To Glasgow & South Western men, this meant that the 'Auld Enemy' had won the last battle, even though there might be a common interest in resisting the English dominance exerted from Euston. Not only (as mentioned earlier) did the Caledonian General Manager become LMS Deputy General Manager for Scotland, but Caley men filled almost all the key Scottish departmental posts: Divisional Locomotive Engineer, Divisional Engineer, (though the Highland retained its own Divisional Engineer), and General Superintendent. An outward and visible sign of Caley dominance was the wholesale slaughter of Glasgow & South Western locomotives and the transfer of that railway's Clyde steamers to the Caledonian Steam Packet Company.

On the LNER side power politics were not so much in evidence. James Calder, the North British General Manager, became General

Manager, Scottish Area, though the GNS section was allowed the dignity of being called Northern Scottish Area until it was eventually downgraded to District status in 1928 and placed under a District Traffic Superintendent, Aberdeen. However, Calder's successors had to accept a rather less grand title, that of Divisional General Manager, while the corresponding LMS post was also redesignated, in this case as Chief Officer for Scotland. That change of name reflected the LMS philosophy, which was to exert control from Euston whenever the option existed, so the Scottish Chief Officer, whatever his local prestige, tended to be more of a spokesman and a local co-ordinator for the railway, rather than a local general manager. The LNER, while reserving some functions to the all-line departments and the Chief General Manager in London, delegated day-to-day management firmly to Edinburgh.

It would be absurd not to admit that the amalgamation brought some benefits to the Scottish railways and especially to the hard-pressed Highland, where locomotives and rolling stock from other sections of the LMS appeared and, a particularly welcome improvement, restaurant cars began to be included in all the principal expresses. An agreeable feature after the grouping was the open mind which many Scottish enginemen preserved on the subject of 'foreign' locomotives that began to appear in their running sheds. Unlike ex-LNWR drivers, for instance, who at first could find nothing good to say of the Midland compounds when they appeared on the Western Division, the more thoughtful Scotsmen on the LMS regarded the unorthodox handling methods required by the compounds as a challenge, and they soon obtained excellent performances. The same applied on the LNER when the first 4–4–0 passenger locomotives of ex-GCR Director class (though with minor modifications to fit the restricted NB loading gauge) were drafted to the Scottish Area, and were properly handled from the start.

One obvious consequence of the grouping was the disappearance of the initials ECJS and WCJS. The East and West Coast joint stock became automatically either LNER or LMS, with the notable exception of the M&NB stock which operated over the Waverley route to Edinburgh. The carriages were divided between the LMS and the LNER with the result that the latter railway acquired some typical Derby-built Midland clerestory vehicles which looked very odd when they were repainted in light brown to simulate the LNER teak finish.

A consequence of the amalgamation that cannot have been welcome to Caledonian loyalists was the LMS decision to discontinue Pullman services which (as the Pullman advertisement in the *Railway Year Book* proudly proclaimed) included 'Dining Cars from Glasgow and Edinburgh to Aberdeen, Carlisle, Oban, Perth, Stirling, Gleneagles . . .' as well as an observation car to Oban in summer, even though the LMS took over the cars and continued to use them for a time.

It is difficult, looking back, to answer the question whether the Scottish lines received a fair crack of the whip, above all in the modernisation of equipment, under the grouping. Outwardly the changes, apart from new engine and passenger carriage liveries, were not very conspicuous for a considerable time. The ex-NB still presented the paradox of a splendid (if draughty!) terminus at Waverley, the great Forth and Tay Bridges, the beautiful Reid Atlantics, together with a lot of dilapidated wayside stations and some pretty dilapidated rolling stock. The Caley was still a solid and self-confident piece of railway; the Highland still struggled manfully with its operating problems and endemic unpunctuality. The GNS still served its corner of the country adequately if unostentatiously.

But there was a certain erosion of standards, as there was in England, due to shortage of money. The splendid, spacious stations which W.A. Paterson, the Caledonian Chief Engineer, had built (and equipped with those famous hanging flower baskets) began to look grubby, and parts of the Sou-West almost dilapidated. On the other hand, some modest strengthening of resources came with, for instance, the drafting of ex-GER Holden B12 4–6–0s to the Great North of Scotland section, for which their low axle-loading made them particularly suitable and where they did excellent work. And when Stanier's Black Fives came to the Highland main line they did splendidly, especially through the second world war.

Memory recalls with pleasure many features of the Scottish railways that survived the grouping. Much was due to the natural dignity and self-respect of so many railwaymen – drivers, firemen, signalmen, ticket collectors, inspectors – who retained a pride in their calling which too often was being eroded south of the Border. In a lonely signalbox on the Highland line, on the footplate of an A3 crossing the Forth Bridge, in a sleeping car talking to the attendant as the train swung round the curve by the Nigg lighthouse into early-morning Aberdeen, conversations with men of great character, personalities in their own right, come to mind. If equipment became shabby, most railwaymen did not.

But it must remain an open question whether a separate Scottish

Railway Company could have continued indefinitely, without any form of subsidy. It might have had to 'do a Beeching' long before the axe fell in the 1960s. The LMS in fact made noises from time to time about the uneconomic character of the ex-Highland Further North main line, and suggested that it was, in principle, a case for subsidy or closure. A Scottish Railway Company would, one may guess, have faced the problems of uneconomic lines or branches in Scotland – the Kyle of Lochalsh line, the Portpatrick & Wigtown-shire line, the many branches of the GNS in Buchan – much as they had to be faced a quarter of a century later, with Scottish pragmatism tempered by an understanding of Scottish social needs. This author, at any rate, believes it would have been better to have tackled these problems in the 1920s and 1930s, than to have shelved them until the 1960s. The LMS and the LNER really had too many other major headaches to worry about the long-term future of the railways in Scotland and their place in the Scottish economy. They did not, perhaps, do too badly for Scotland, but probably Scotland would have done better for herself with a Scottish Railway Company.

APPENDIX 2

The Irish Enclaves

Although all the companies had overseas offices and ticket agencies, it was only in Ireland that two of them owned railway installations outside Great Britain. Naturally, the railways concerned were those with shipping interests across the Irish Sea – the LMS and the Great Western.

By far the most important was the part of the LMS in Ulster managed by that railway's Northern Counties Committee, which was a legacy from the Midland Railway. Always restlessly extending its tentacles, the Midland had purchased the Belfast & Northern Counties Railway in 1903. The purchase was logical since the Midland was interested in the Portpatrick & Wigtownshire Joint Railway (the other partners being the LNWR, the Caledonian and the Glasgow & South Western) and thus in the shortest sea route to Ireland, from Stranraer to Larne, with 80 per cent owned by the Portpatrick & Wigtownshire and 20 per cent by the Belfast & Northern Counties Railway. The Midland was moreover about to open its own shipping route from Heysham to Belfast. The Belfast & Northern Counties purchase was timely and gave the Midland control not only of the rail route from Larne to Belfast but also of the main line linking the two principal cities of Ulster, Belfast and Londonderry, 202 miles of broad (5ft 3in) gauge line as well as 31 miles of narrow (3ft) gauge.

By this purchase, the Midland also acquired the share, previously held by the B&NCR jointly with the Great Northern Railway of Ireland, in the extensive network of narrow-gauge lines known as the County Donegal Railway, with 91 miles of route directly owned and operated. The Midland also had hotels in Belfast, Larne and Portrush.

The Midland appointed a 'Secretary and Manager' (later, in LMS days, a Manager) with headquarters in Belfast, to control the railway under the policy guidance of the Northern Counties Committee, which gave its name, rather than that of the Midland, to the system. But the Midland, and afterwards the LMS, kept the NCC on a fairly tight rein from headquarters. The locomotives were, even though of 5ft 3in gauge, typical Derby products for many years.

It was never a very prosperous concern; its capital expenditure was included in that of the parent system and it only managed to earn relatively small net receipts before the LMS was nationalised. Its rolling stock then included 59 locomotives, 183 passenger carriages including restaurant cars, and 2,136 wagons on the broad gauge – but only 4 locomotives and 6 carriages on the narrow! It was transferred to the Ulster Transport Authority, together with its rolling stock, repair shops and hotels, soon after the LMS was nationalised, the compensation paid to the British Transport Commission being £2,668,000.

Another LMS system in Ireland was far removed from the main line character of the NCC. When the London & North Western Railway in 1872 opened its shipping service from Holyhead to Greenore, it provided the capital for two short stretches of railway. The first, opened in 1873, was the Dundalk & Greenore Railway which connected with the Irish North Western Railway at Dundalk. For its train services, the LNWR built rolling stock at Crewe and Wolverton to the Irish broad gauge which was shipped to Ireland. Immediately afterwards the D&GR put in hand the construction of a second line, from Greenore to Newry, to shorten the distance to Belfast, the company's name then being changed to Dundalk, Newry & Greenore. The LNWR also built a substantial hotel at Greenore to help popularise the route.

This small railway, with 27 miles of route, came into the hands of the LMS at the grouping. However, the DN&G operated at a loss for years (the position being aggravated by the partition of Ireland and the institution of customs and border controls between Greenore and Newry) well before the LMS was nationalised. Its train services were discontinued after the end of 1951, the assets, including 5 locomotives, 10 carriages – all genuine LNWR relics – and a couple of diesel cars, as well as the hotel, being sold off by the British Transport Commission.

A third LMS enclave was at North Wall, Dublin. Here, alongside the steamer berths on the River Liffey, the LNWR had provided a passenger station, hotel, goods station, lairage for cattle, and a large fleet of road vehicles for local collection and delivery. From North Wall, a length of LNWR line, built to the 5ft 3in gauge, connected with the Irish railway system proper through Church Road Junctions. However, in 1920, the LNWR, after years of struggle, wrested the mail contract from the competing City of Dublin Steam Packet Co, which went out of business. In due course, passenger traffic was concentrated at Kingstown (Dun Laoghaire) and the North Wall

211

berths were used solely by the cargo and livestock ships to Holy-head. The passenger station provided a welcome addition to the freight facilities, especially useful for storing consignments awaiting clearance by the Irish Customs; the hotel ultimately became the offices of the LMS Irish Traffic Manager.

The fourth Irish enclave was the Fishguard & Rosslare Railways & Harbours Company which for most of the period of the grouping was jointly owned by the Great Western Railway of England and the Great Southern Railways of Ireland. The origin of this company was the activity of two speculators who in 1892/3 reactivated several dormant schemes for short railways connecting Rosslare Harbour with Wexford and Waterford on the Irish side, for extending harbour works at Fishguard and connecting them with the Great Western on the Welsh side. The GWR in 1899, jointly with the (then) Great Southern & Western Railway of Ireland, obtained control of the Fishguard & Rosslare Railways & Harbours Company, the Welsh portion of the railway together with the harbour and hotel at Fishguard being managed by the GWR. The Irish section of 104 miles as far as Fermoy, together with Rosslare Harbour, was worked by the GSWR, although connections were made at Wexford and at Waterford with the Dublin & South Eastern Railway.

The Company also owned the steamers on the Fishguard–Rosslare route, of which there were three up to the outbreak of the first world war. They were managed by the GWR and in fact one of these ships (by agreement) was transferred during the summer to the GWR Channel Islands service from Weymouth.

After 1924 and the Irish railway amalgamations, the GSWR and the DSER (together with the other principal systems in what was then the Irish Free State, now the Republic) were merged in the Great Southern Railways. In 1945 the GSR was itself merged in Coras Iompair Eireann (Irish Transport Company), which has continued to hold the capital in the Fishguard & Rosslare Company previously owned by the GSR, the GWR share being transferred to the British Transport Commission on nationalisation in 1948.

APPENDIX 3
The Joint Lines

One effect of the 1923 grouping was considerably to reduce the large number of jointly-owned sections of railway, since many had been joint between companies now grouped together. Even so, the old names sometimes continued in daily use, a good example being the Great Northern & Great Eastern Joint Line from March to Black Carr Junction, Doncaster, which became purely LNER at the grouping but which to this day is still known to BR's Eastern Region railwaymen as 'the Joint Line'.

The post-1923 joint lines fell into two main categories: railways operating their own train services, and sections of line or stations jointly owned for use by the parent companies. The former class comprised the Cheshire Lines Railway, managed by the Cheshire Lines Committee (33⅓ per cent LMS, ex-Midland, and 66⅔ per cent LNER, ex-GCR and ex-GNR); the Somerset & Dorset Joint Railway (50 per cent LMS, ex-Midland, and 50 per cent Southern, ex-LSWR); and the Midland & Great Northern Joint Railway (50 per cent LMS and 50 per cent LNER).

Practices on these railways varied considerably. The CLC (143 route-miles) owned its own passenger rolling stock (288 vehicles in 1938) but no wagons, apart from service vehicles. Traction for its domestic services was provided by the LNER, a legacy from GCR days, though through trains from the LMS and LNER were worked by the engines of those companies.

It had two main lines, from Manchester to Liverpool and from Manchester to Chester, together with a suburban route (owned by a subsidiary company) from Liverpool to Southport. Its only express services were the hourly 45-minute Manchester–Liverpool fliers; the Chester trains were of very secondary character. Its main source of prosperity was the heavy freight traffic it carried from and to various exchange points with the parent companies, particularly the Midland and the Great Central at Cheadle and Godley respectively.

The Somerset & Dorset (103 route-miles) operated a fleet of loco-motives as well as passenger carriages in its own blue livery until 1930, when the locomotives were taken over by the LMS and the rolling stock was divided between the LMS and the Southern.

213

Thereafter the LMS was responsible for traction and rolling stock, the civil engineering side being undertaken by the Southern. Train services over the long, straggling main line from Bath to Bournemouth (with a long branch to Burnham-on-Sea) were not exactly speedy, but heavy summer holiday traffic, including the Pines Express from Manchester to Bournemouth, demanded a high standard of locomotive performance over a hilly route. Its finances were hampered by lack of a really remunerative freight traffic until the second world war, when it became an important north–south route for military supplies and its capacity was taxed to the full, for a few brief years.

The Midland & Great Northern Joint Railway had no less than 183 route-miles of its own and in addition was a joint owner with the LNER of the Norfolk & Suffolk Joint line of 22 route-miles, linking Yarmouth and Lowestoft (originally joint between the M&GN and GER). The M&GN was for many years a most distinctive railway, with its locomotive livery of yellow-brown and its own miniature Swindon or Crewe in the shape of its excellent repair shops at Melton Constable.

The Midland Railway assumed responsibility for locomotive provision in 1893 and thereafter Derby designs became ubiquitous on the M&GN, although painted in the line's own livery. But in 1936 the LNER assumed responsibility for operation and traction and the M&GN engines were absorbed into the stock of that parent company. The M&GN had 156 passenger carriages just before the second world war, though, like the CLC and the S&DJR, it owned no wagons other than service vehicles.

Its long main line, rather like a letter Y with two stems joining to form a single route of mostly single track from Bourne and Peterborough through South Lynn to Cromer, and Yarmouth with a branch to Norwich, saw some spirited locomotive performances, particularly with summer holiday through trains from the Midland towns to the Norfolk coast. It was notable for some operating feats in passing two trains in opposite directions, both of which were longer than the passing loop!

A short line that owned its own passenger stock (68 vehicles in 1938) was the Manchester South Junction & Altrincham line (LMS and LNER), no more than 9 miles long, electrified by the parent companies in 1931.

The many other post-1923 joint lines showed great diversity. There were also many stations in joint ownership, though in Britain the American practice of railways clubbing together to build an imposing Union Station in the centre of a city had never taken root.

The non-operating joint lines were usually managed by a committee principally concerned with the accountancy arrangements for recording user of the track, and services such as civil engineering maintenance performed by the parent companies. Maintenance was sometimes divided on a geographical basis, sometimes carried out for the joint line as a whole by each parent in rotation.

As might be expected, two of the cross-London lines were joint. The West London from Willesden (LMS) and Old Oak Common (GWR) to Kensington (Addison Road) – Olympia after 1946 – was jointly owned by the LMS and the GWR; the West London Extension from Kensington to Clapham Junction on the Southern was owned by the two previous railways plus the Southern.

The East London line had a complicated history and a complicated pattern of ownership. It started from a junction with the LNER just outside Liverpool Street Station and then, with a spur from the Metropolitan and District Joint Line between St Mary's and Whitechapel, proceeded under the Thames through Sir Marc Isambard Brunel's original and ill-starred Thames Tunnel to link up with the Southern's Brighton line at New Cross Gate and with the South Eastern main line at New Cross. Soon after grouping, in 1925, ownership was transferred to the Southern but the line was leased to a Joint Committee of the Southern, the LNER, the Metropolitan and the District, the two latter being of course merged in the LPTB in 1933.

The North & South Western Junction Railway from Willesden Junction to Kew on the Southern Railway Hounslow loop, although constructed as a joint line by the LNWR and the LSWR, was leased in its entirety to the LMS and therefore scarcely ranks as joint.

There were several joint lines shared by one or other of the main line companies and one of the railways that in 1933 became part of the London Passenger Transport Board. The Metropolitan and Great Central Joint Committee administered 46 miles of route between Harrow South Junction, Aylesbury and Verney Junction with branches to Chesham and Brill, and, later, to Watford. The Metropolitan operated its trains over the whole system, the LNER over the greater part. The Hammersmith & City Railway, only three miles long, had rolling stock identical with that of the Metropolitan (which worked the line) but distinguished by being labelled 'Great Western and Metropolitan' to identify ownership.

One may wonder why the railways could not agree to get rid of the cumbrous management and accountancy arrangements connected with the joint lines. There certainly was a tendency in the case of the operating joint railways to scale down the functions of the local management and, on grounds of economy, to transfer work to one or other of the parent companies. This did not always have the happiest results. There was often a loss of morale among staff due to the remoteness of the new bosses and a certain reluctance among the parent railway departments to allocate much managerial attention to a minor system that was not wholly owned.

The post-war plans of the railway companies included an intention to eliminate the joint lines by progressive absorption in one or other parent undertaking. In the event, this of course happened under nationalisation when Regional boundaries were created or adjusted, apart from those lines joint with London Transport. The process here took a good deal longer to complete. The last major transfer was when the Metropolitan & Great Central Joint line was divided, the section from Amersham to Aylesbury passing to British Railways and the section from Harrow South Junction to Amersham to London Transport.

APPENDIX 4
Bibliography

Comprehensive histories of the four great railways are not many, although the mechanical engineering side has been covered by a plethora of books dealing with most aspects of steam locomotive development and passenger carriage design, as well as with train running performance.

But the LNER has been admirably described by Cecil J. Allen in *The London and North Eastern Railway.* For many years the doyen of writers in his own field, Allen did not allow his special interest in the steam locomotive to prevent him from writing a comprehensive and well balanced history of his own Company.

The Great Western has also been well covered by E.T. MacDermot's classic *History of the Great Western Railway,* to which O.S. Nock has added a third volume carrying the story up to nationalisation.

The LMS has been vividly pictured by C. Hamilton Ellis in his entertaining book *London Midland and Scottish* which is really more of an engineering history than a Company history, though it contains some fascinating character sketches of individual LMS officers and sidelights on many of that great railway's practices.

The Southern is the subject of two large works, but C.F. Dendy Marshall's *History of the Southern Railway,* usefully updated to 1939 by R.W. Kidner, is rather misleadingly titled, since the greater part of the book deals with the histories of the constituent companies that only became the Southern Railway in 1923. And C.F. Klapper's *Sir Herbert Walker's Southern Railway,* although a mine of information, well presented, is linked (as its title suggests) to one man's managerial achievements; Walker retired from the general managership (though becoming a director) ten years before the Southern was nationalised.

A vast amount of information – geographical as well as historical – is contained in the series of *Regional Histories of the Railways of Great Britain,* by various authors, which give plenty of attention to the railways after 1923, though of course on a regional rather than a company basis.

O.S. Nock's *Scottish Railways* and H.C. Casserley's *Britain's Joint Lines* are valuable subsidiary sources.

The organisation of the four main line railways is covered by M.R. Bonavia, *The Organisation of British Railways*.

A good summary of management problems (based on the LMS) is *Railways* by W.V. Wood and Sir Josiah Stamp; a public relations volume on the same railway's achievements is *A British Railway behind the Scenes* by J.W. Williamson.

A fully comprehensive history of railway shipping services has yet to be written, but the ground has been covered to a considerable extent in Duckworth and Langmuir's *Railway and Other Steamers*.

Chapters dealing critically with the grouped railways' policies are included in D.H. Aldcroft's *British Railways in Transition*, in T.C. Barker and C.A. Savage, *An Economic History of Transport in Britain*, and in P.S. Bagwell, *The Transport Revolution from 1770*.

A valuable account of railway trade unionism is given in P.S. Bagwell's *The Railwaymen*, the official history of the National Union of Railwaymen.

Various authors produced semi-polemical books and pamphlets dealing with railway financial problems and the question of road-rail co-ordination between the wars, but nowadays they are of only minor interest.

The railway companies commissioned their own accounts, by various authors, of their achievements during the second world war; there is also the authoritative and factual *History of the British Railways during the Second World War, 1939–45* by Robert Bell, and the popular all-company history, *Timetable for Victory*, by Evan John, as well as O.S. Nock's *Britain's Railways at War*.

Nationalisation of the railways has generally been treated by writers as one component (and not the most controversial one) in the nationalisation of public transport under the Transport Act 1947. The fullest factual account is contained in Sir Norman Chester's massive volume, *The Nationalisation of British Industry, 1945–50*. A shorter and less objective sketch is included in R. Kelf-Cohen's *Twenty Years of Nationalisation*.

There is still a great deal of research to be done into policy formation and management attitudes on the railways, using the Minute Books and other papers of the companies as well as the files of the Ministry of Transport, now in the Public Record Office, and all, under the 30 years rule, open for study by bona fide students of railway history.

Index

Note: References to individual railway companies have been omitted, as these are very numerous and the chapter headings indicate the subjects covered. A good many locomotive types are referred to in Chapters 2 to 6, but are not individually indexed below.

INDEX

Wood, Sir William, 14, 27, 32, 35, 196
Worsdell, Wilson, 92
Pickfords, 126, 130, 155, 156, 158, 173
Plaistow Works, 155
Post Office, 21
Pullman services, 50, 65, 84, 107, 108, 109, 208

Railway Advisory Committee, 14
Railway Air Services, 164, 173
Railway Benevolent Institution, 151
Railway Clearing House, 5, 8, 169, 170, 172
Railway Clerks Association, 146, 149
Railway Companies Association, 12, 148, 172, 173, 195, 199
Railway Convalescent Homes, 151
Railway Control Agreements, 182, 193, 195
Railway Executive, 11, 36
Railway Executive Committee, 9, 10, 173, 185, 186, 187, 197
Railway Finance Corporation, 68, 143, 182
Railway Passenger Duty, 181
Railway Rates Tribunal, 130, 180
Railways Act 1921, 5, 16, 18, 23, 130, 147, 173, 176
Railways Staff Conference, 148
Regulation of the Forces Act 1871, 8
'Reliostop', 114
Road Haulage Association, 132, 195
Road Traffic Act 1930, 129
Road and Rail Traffic Act 1933, 129
Royal Commission on Transport, 129

SPD Ltd, 131
Scottish Motor Transport Group, 157
Sectional councils, 147
Sheffield Joint Omnibus Committee, 157
Southampton (port), 85, 163
Spartan Air Lines, 164
'Square Deal' campaign, 132, 173
Spiers & Pond (caterers), 84, 166

Standing Joint Committee (LPTB & railways), 172
Stations
Aldermaston, 186
Banbury, 52
Berwick, 137
Blackfriars, 167
Clacton, 137
Doncaster, 134
Down Street (LT), 186
Euston, 6, 28, 134, 136, 144
Exeter (St David's), 52, 144
Felixstowe, 135
Gloucester, 52
Grantham, 134
Horley, 135
Huddersfield, 134
Kilburn High Road, 135
King's Cross, 7, 135, 136
Leeds (Central), 134
Leeds (City), 34
London Bridge, 186
Newcastle (Central), 57, 135
Oxford, 52
Paddington, 6
Peterborough, 134
Plymouth (North Road), 144
Preston, 134
Reading (GW), 52
Retford, 134
St Pancras, 22, 134
Slough, 52
Streatham Common, 135
Taunton, 52
Waterloo, 74, 186
Waverley (Edinburgh), 135
Wemyss Bay, 134
York, 57, 135
Swindon Works, 155, 193

Tilling Group, 157
Towle Dynasty, 166
Trains (named)
Atlantic Coast Express, 47, 82
Bournemouth Belle, 82, 108
Brighton Belle, 82, 108
Bristolian, 46, 111

222

INDEX

223